CROSSROADS 1

Workbook

Marjorie Fuchs

with
Irene Frankel
Cliff Meyers

Oxford University Press

Oxford University Press

198 Madison Avenue
New York, NY 10016

Great Clarendon Street
Oxford OX2 6DP England

Oxford New York
Auckland Bangkok Buenos Aires Cape Town Chennai
Dar es Salaam Delhi Hong Kong Istanbul Karachi Kolkata
Kuala Lumpur Madrid Melbourne Mexico City Mumbai Nairobi
São Paulo Shanghai Singapore Taipei Tokyo Toronto

with an associated company in Berlin

OXFORD is a trademark of Oxford University Press.

ISBN 0-19-434528-9

Senior Editor: Ellen Lehrburger
Editor: Ken Mencz
Design Manager: Lynn Luchetti
Art Buyer/Picture Researcher: Paula Radding
Production Manager: Shanta Persaud
Cover illustration by Dennis Ziemienski.
Interior illustrations by Susan Detrich, Leslie Dunlap, Doug Jamieson, Jody Jobe, John Jones,
Karin Kretschmann, Bob Marstall, Frank Magadan, Mary Martylewski, Shelley Matheis, Stephanie
O'Shaughnessy, and Joel Snyder.
Production and Design by Rita Myers, Lise Prown, and Paul Rodriguez, Function Thru Form. Inc.
Realia by Guilbert Gates, Kathleen Katims, Leslie Nolan, and Stephan Van Litsenborg.
Printing (last digit): 10 9 8
Printed in China

Acknowledgments

We wish to thank:

Dan Rabideau of the Literacy Assistance Center and
Jim Roth of the City University of New York, for their
valuable insights into the needs of students not literate
in English, and for their creative ideas on working with
multilevel classes.

Fiona Armstrong of the New York City Board of
Education, Mally Ramos, Connie Sommer, and Jim Roth
of the City University of New York, and Chito Adienza of
the YMCA Elisair program, for generously sharing their
classrooms and ideas.

Shirley Brod of the Spring Institute for International
Studies and Christine Bunn of the City College of San
Francisco, for their helpful comments on our
manuscript.

Our editors at Oxford University Press: Susan Lanzano,
for getting us started; Ellen Lehrburger, for seeing us
through; and Ken Mencz, for working so painstakingly
and with such unfailing good humor on the final
manuscript. We would also like to thank the rest of the
Oxford University Press staff, especially Jane
Sturtevant, Paul Phillips, and Jim O'Connor for all their
help and support.

Marjorie Fuchs
Irene Frankel
Cliff Meyers

Table of Contents

Cross-Reference to Crossroads 1 Student Book

Cross-Reference to Crossroads 1 Student Book

<table>
<tr><td>

UNIT 6
Grammar (Levels A and B)

Writing (Levels A and B)

Punctuation

Game: "B" Search

</td><td>

Use After Student Book
Page 64
Exercise 10

Page 68
Exercise 7

Page 70
Exercise 2

Page 70
Exercise 2

</td></tr>
</table>

UNIT 7
Grammar (Levels A and B) — Page 76, Exercise 13

Writing (Levels A and B) — Page 80, Exercise 6

Capitalization and Punctuation — Page 82, Exercise 1

Crossword Puzzle — Page 82, Exercise 1

UNIT 8
Grammar (Levels A and B) — Page 87, Exercise 9

Crossword Puzzle — Page 89, Exercise 4

Writing (Levels A and B) — Page 90, Exercise 3

Capitalization — Page 90, Exercise 3

UNIT 9
Grammar (Levels A and B) — Page 100, Exercise 10

Writing (Levels A and B) — Page 104, Exercise 6

Punctuation — Page 106, Exercise 2

Game: Word Search — Page 106, Exercise 2

UNIT 10
Grammar (Levels A and B) — Page 112, Exercise 11

Crossword Puzzle — Page 113, Exercise 4

Writing (Levels A and B) — Page 118, Exercise 2

Punctuation — Page 118, Exercise 2

UNIT 1

Grammar   Level A

1. Circle.

a.

He (She)

b.

He   She

c.

He   She

d.

He   She

2. Match.

a. she is   you're

b. I am   he's

c. he is   I'm

d. you are   she's

3. Complete.

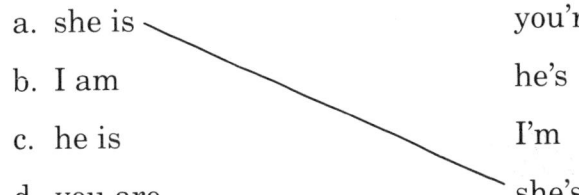

| His | Her | He's | She's |

 ___His___ name is Han Fu.
___He's___ from China.

a.

 _____ name is Sara.
_____ from the United States.

b.

 _____ name is Victor.
_____ from Colombia.

c.

 _____ name is Neary.
_____ from Cambodia.

d.

4. Complete.

| Where are | What's |

a. ___What's___ your first name?

b. _____ your last name?

c. _____ you from?

Grammar

Level B

1. Write the contractions.

a. He is _____He's_____

b. I am _____

c. She is _____

d. You are _____

2. Complete. Use the contractions in 1.

Hi. ___I'm___ Neary.
a.

_____ from Cambodia.
b.

And this is Victor.

_____ from Colombia.
c.

Hi. This is Anna

_____ from Poland.
d.

Hi.

3. Write the sentences.

Her	His

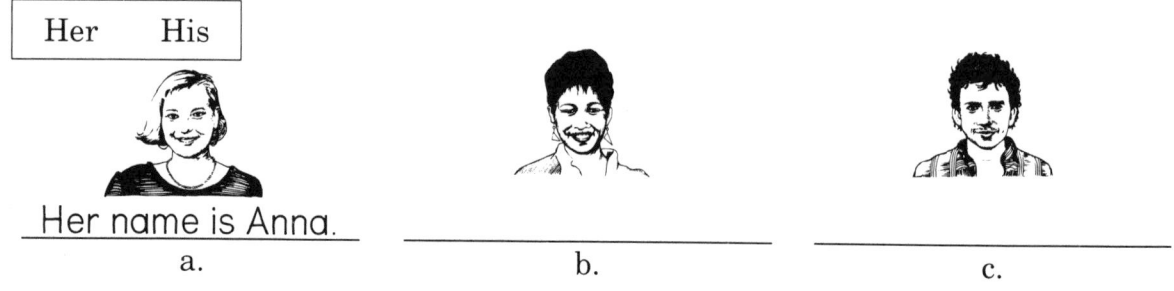

Her name is Anna.
a.

_____
b.

_____
c.

4. Complete.

a. _____What's_____ your first name?

b. _____ your last name?

c. _____ are you from?

5. Answer the questions in 4.

a. _____

b. _____

c. _____

Writing   Level A

1. Circle (Name).

Red Cross

HOSPITAL AND SURGICAL-MEDICAL CONTRACTS

SUBSCRIBER'S (NAME) (LAST, FIRST)

IDENTIFICATION

a.

VIC'S

V I D E O

PREPAID RENTAL CERTIFICATE

Good for _____ Movies

Name _____

b.

Facts to Remember	NAME	NAME	NAME
Birthday			
Anniversary			
Shirt/Blouse Size			
Sweater			

c.

Dr. Tahira Homayun
2001 University Avenue
Madison, Wisconsin 53705

Name _____

Next Appointment _____

d.

(Continued on page 4)

Writing

Level A (continued)

2. Circle (First).
Underline Last.

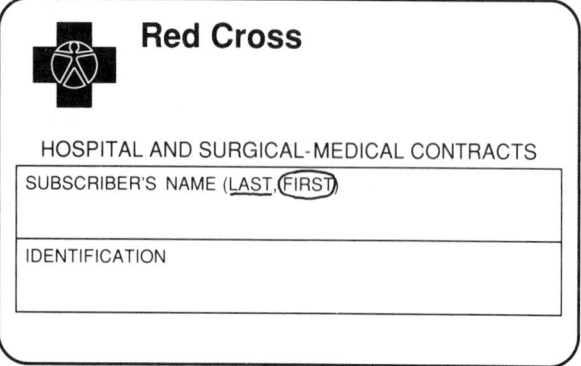

a.

b.

c.

d.

3. Look at 1a, 1b, 2b, 2c, and 2d.
Write your first and last name.

Writing   **Level B**

---

1. Complete.

| is   meet   ~~name~~   Nice   too |

A: Hi. I'm Rosa. What's your _____name_____?
   a.

B: My name _____ Han Fu.
                b.

A: Nice to _____ you, Han Fu.
              c.

B: _____ to meet you, _____.
        d.   e.

2. Meet Anna.
   Complete.

You: _____Hi_____. I'm _____. What's _____ name?
            a.   b.   c.

Anna: My _____ _____ Anna.
              d.   e.

You: Nice to _____ _____, Anna.
                    f.   g.

Anna: _____ _____ meet _____, too.
              h.   i.   j.

3. Meet Victor.
   Write a conversation.

You: _____

Victor: _____

You: _____

Victor: _____

Punctuation

1. Add punctuation.

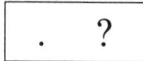

Victor: Hi. I'm Victor.

What's your name

Anna: My name is Anna

Victor: I'm from Colombia

Where are you from, Anna

Anna: I'm from Poland

Victor: Nice to meet you, Anna

Anna: Nice to meet you, too

2. Copy the conversation in 1.

Victor: ___Hi. I'm Victor._____

_____

Anna: _____

Victor: _____

_____

Anna: _____

Victor: _____

Anna: _____

Crossword Puzzle

Levels A and B

1. Complete the puzzle.

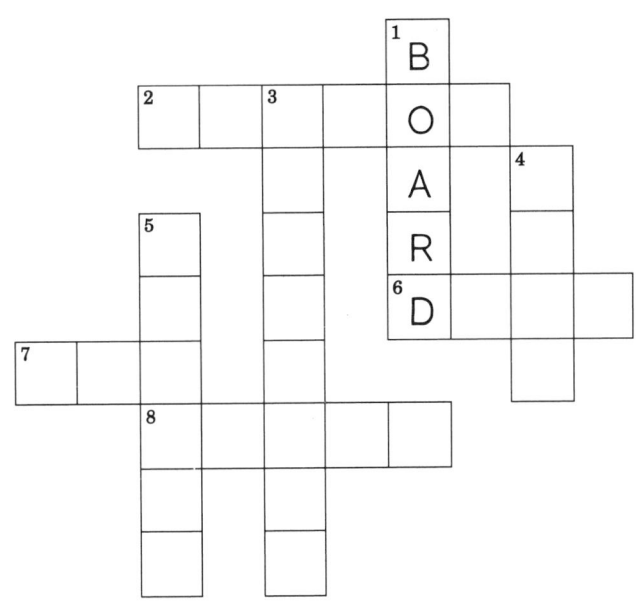

Across ➡

2. (window)

6. (door)

7. (pen)

8. (clock)

Down ⬇

1. (board)

3. (notebook)

4. (book)

5. (pencil)

1. Match.

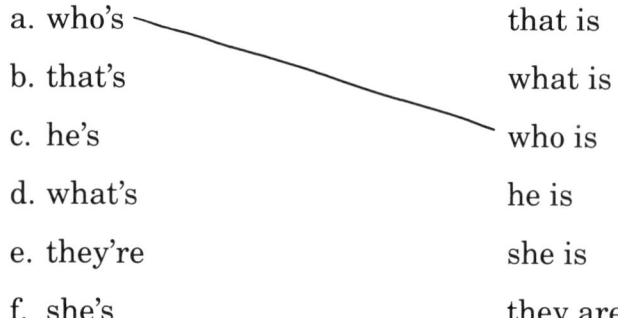

a. who's   that is

b. that's   what is

c. he's   who is

d. what's   he is

e. they're   she is

f. she's   they are

2. Complete.

Who	~~Who's~~	What	What's	That's	They're	she	she's

A: ____Who's____ that?
    a.

B: _____ my sister.
    b.

A: _____ her name?
    c.

B: Neary.

A: Is _____ married?
     d.

B: No, _____ not.
     e.

A: _____ are those people?
    f.

B: _____ my friends.
    g.

A: _____ are their names?
    h.

B: Rosa and Anna.

Grammar   **Level B**

1. **Write the contractions.**

   a. who is _____who's_____

   b. that is _____

   c. what is _____

   d. they are _____

   e. she is _____

   f. he is _____

2. **Complete.**

   A: _____Who's_____ that?
           a.

   B: That's my brother.

   A: And who's _____?
                  b.

   B: _____ my sister.
         c.

   A: _____ her name?
         d.

   B: Neary.

   A: Is she married?

   B: No, _____ _____.
           e.   f.

   A: Is your brother married?

   B: _____, he _____. That's his wife.
         g.   h.

Writing   Level A

1. Circle (Name).

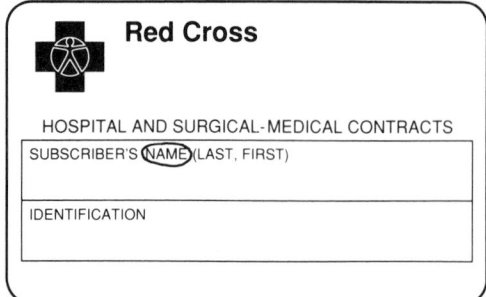

Red Cross HOSPITAL AND SURGICAL-MEDICAL CONTRACTS SUBSCRIBER'S (NAME) (LAST, FIRST) IDENTIFICATION	PLANT ROUTE NUMBER **14** ACCOUNT NUMBER **Q9380** RECEIPT NUMBER **42988** PRINT LAST NAME INITIAL FOR LAB USE ONLY ADDRESS CITY DATE PHONE

a.   b.

2. Underline <u>Phone</u>.

Please send me more information about
the courses or services I've checked.

Name _____

Phone _____

Address _____

City _____ State _____ Zip _____

a.

Vacation

R E G I S T R A T I O N

Date _____

(Area code) Home Phone (_____) _____

Name _____

Address _____

City _____ State _____ Zip _____

b.

(Continued on page 11)

Writing

Level A (continued)

3. Circle (Area Code).

IDENTIFICATION CARD

Name_____

Address_____

City_____ State_____

Area Code_____ Phone_____

In case of accident please notify_____

_____

a.

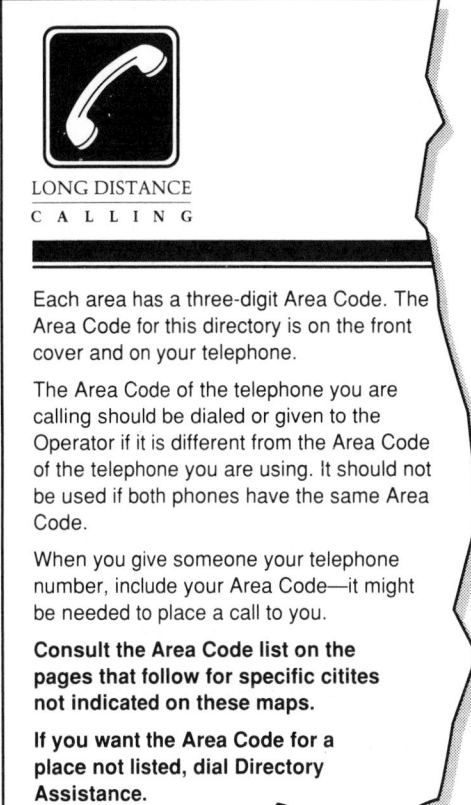

LONG DISTANCE
C A L L I N G

Each area has a three-digit Area Code. The Area Code for this directory is on the front cover and on your telephone.

The Area Code of the telephone you are calling should be dialed or given to the Operator if it is different from the Area Code of the telephone you are using. It should not be used if both phones have the same Area Code.

When you give someone your telephone number, include your Area Code—it might be needed to place a call to you.

Consult the Area Code list on the pages that follow for specific citites not indicated on these maps.

If you want the Area Code for a place not listed, dial Directory Assistance.

b.

4. Look at 1a, 1b, 2a, 2b, and 3a. Write your name.
   Look at 2a, 2b, and 3a. Write your phone number and area code.

Writing   Level B

1. **Complete.**

   A: W<u>h</u> <u>o</u> a<u>r</u> <u>e</u> those people?
         a.   b.

   B: They're my friends.

   A: W__ __ __ a__ __ t __ __ __ __ n __ __ __ __?
         c.   d.   e.   f.

   B: His name is Pablo. Her name is Carmen.

   A: W__ __ __ __ a __ __ t__ __ __ f__ __ __?
         g.   h.   i.   j.

   B: They're from Mexico.

2. **Draw a picture of two (2) classmates. Write their names.**

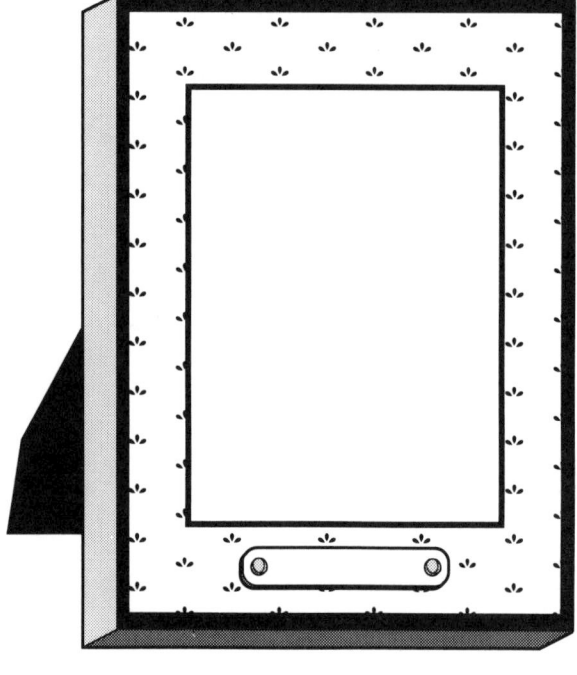

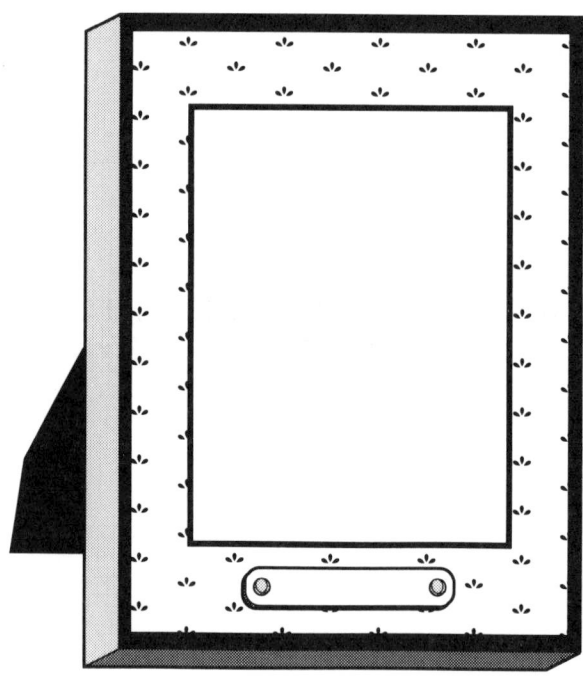

_____   _____

(Continued on page 13)

Writing Level B (continued)

3. **Write about your friends in 2.**

This is a picture of my friends.
This is my friend,
And this is my friend,
         is from
And   is from

Capitalization

1. Put in capital letters.

T
/this is my friend.

her name is sara blanca.

she's from mexico.

this is ana.

ana is sara's daughter.

this is carlos.

he's ana's husband.

Sara   Ana   Carlos

2. Copy the story in 1.

    This is my friend. _____

_____

_____

_____

_____

_____

Crossword Puzzle

1. Look at Mary's family.

Mary's Family

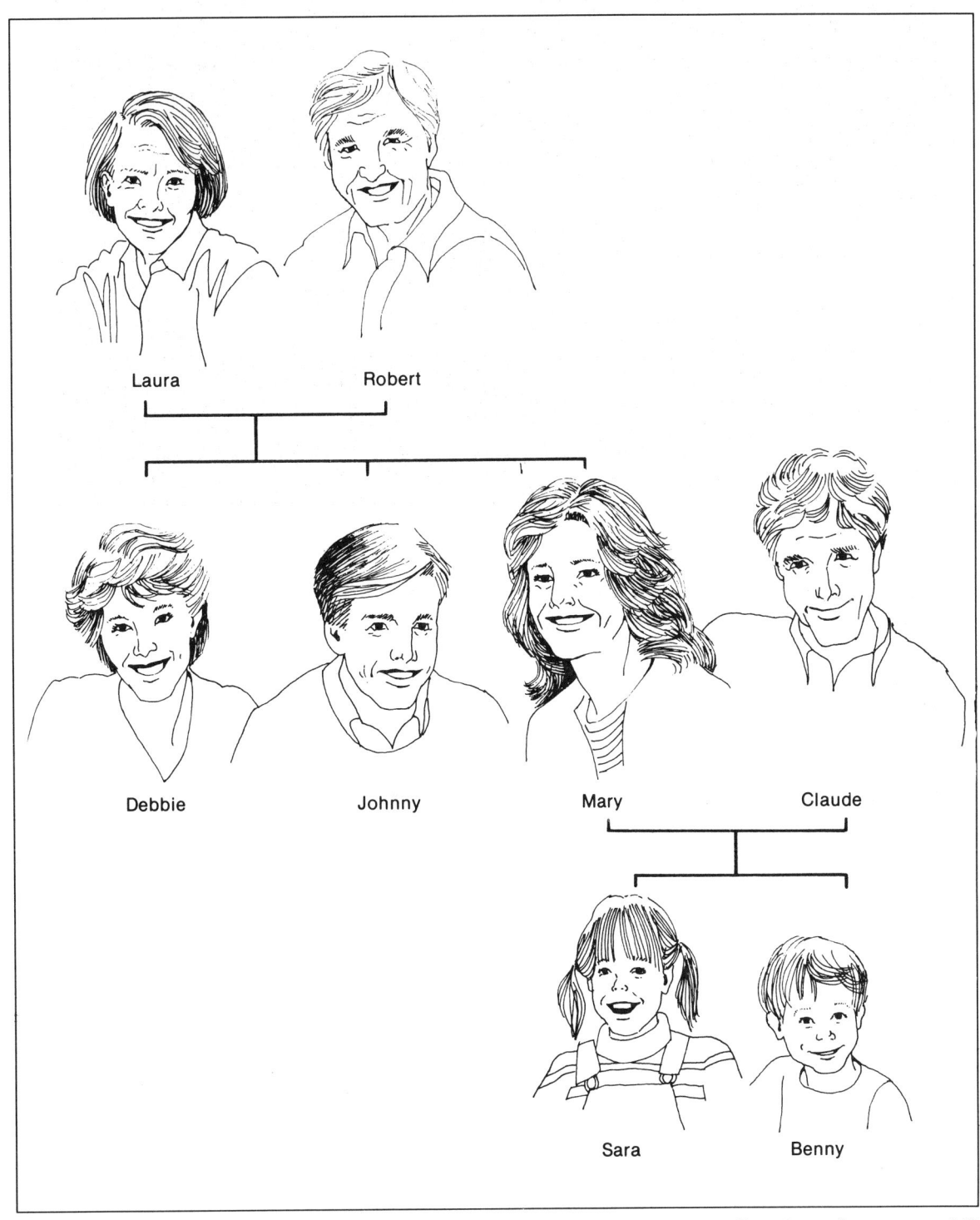

(Continued on page 16)

2. Complete the puzzle.

Across ➡️

3. Laura
6. Debbie
8. Claude
9. Sara
10. Claude and Mary are_____.

Down ⬇️

1. Bob
2. Johnny
4. Mary is Claude's_____.
5. Benny
7. This is Mary's_____.

UNIT 3

Name _____
First   Last

Teacher _____

Grammar   Level A

1. Circle.

a.   (It)   They

b.   It   They

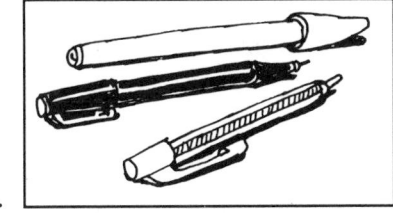

c.   It   They

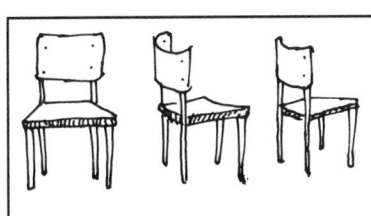

d.   It   They

e.   It   They

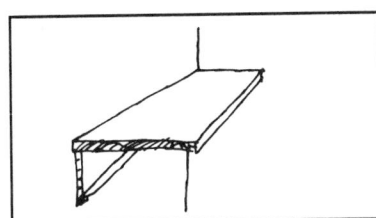

f.   It   They

(Continued on page 18)

Grammar   **Level A (continued)**

2. Circle.

a.    It's on the desk.   (Yes)   No

b.    It's on the floor.   Yes   No

c.    They're on the chair.   Yes   No

d. 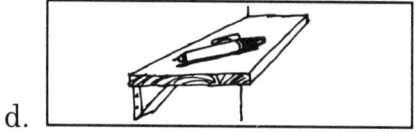   It's on the desk.   Yes   No

3. Complete.

It's   They're

a.    ___They're___ on the shelf.

b.    _____ next to the window.

c.    _____ on the desk.

d.    _____ on the floor.

Grammar   Level B

1. Complete.

a. Are you a new student?

No, I'm not.

b. Are you from Colombia?

c. Are you married?

d. Are you on your break now?

2. Write about yourself. Answer the questions in 1.

a. _____

b. _____

c. _____

d. _____

(Continued on page 20)

Grammar

Level B (continued)

3. Complete.

A: Excuse me. Are you a teacher?

B: N o, I'm n o t. I'm a student.
    a.   b.   c.

A: Oh. Who's y___ ___ ___ teacher?
             d.

B: Sara Gilbert.

A: A___ ___ y___ ___ in Level 1?
     e.   f.

B: N___, I'___ n___ ___. I'm in Level 2.
    g.   h.   i.

A: I'm in Level 1. This is my husband.

   He's in Level 1, too. H___ ___ teacher is David Walker.
                      j.

B: Hi. Nice to meet you. W___ ___ ___ ___ are you from?
                      k.

A and C: W___'___ ___ from Senegal.
          l.

B: Senegal? Is your first language Wolof?

C: Yes, i___ i___. Oh. It's 9:00! We're late.
      m.   n.

   Where is Room 101?

B: Room 101? I___'___ next to the office.
             o.

C: Thanks.

Writing   Level A

1. Circle (number).

   Circle (single).

   Underline married.

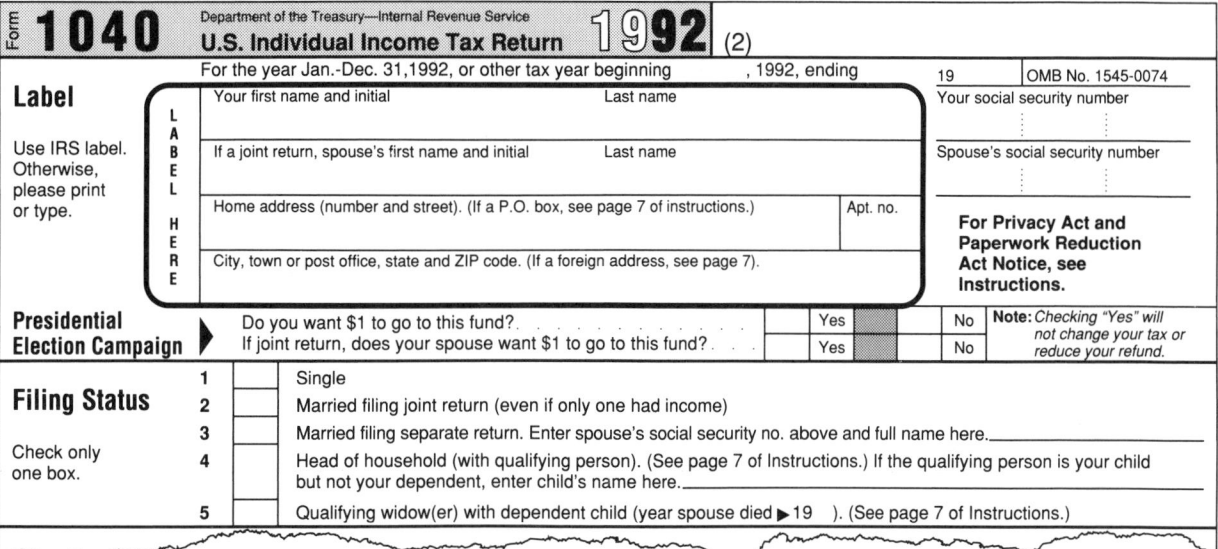

2. Write your first name on the form in 1.
   Write your last name on the form in 1.

Writing   Level B

1. Read the form.

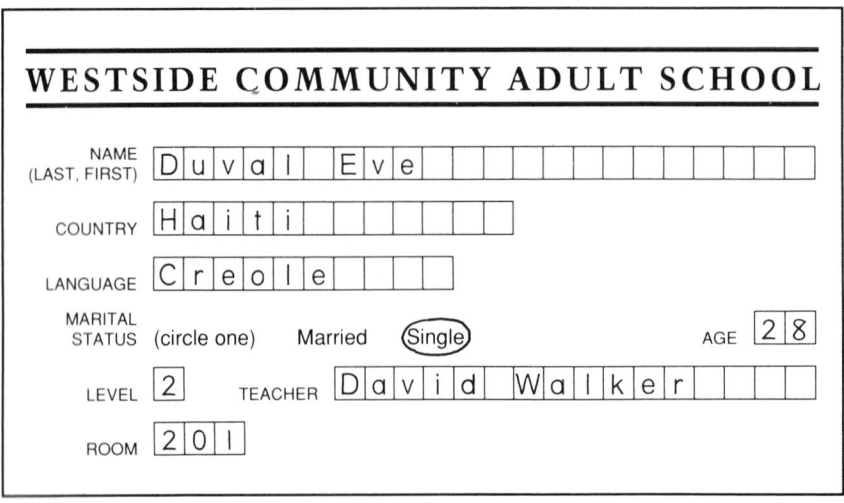

WESTSIDE COMMUNITY ADULT SCHOOL

NAME (LAST, FIRST)	D u v a l　E v e
COUNTRY	H a i t i
LANGUAGE	C r e o l e

MARITAL STATUS (circle one)　Married　(Single)　　　　AGE ⟨2⟩⟨8⟩

LEVEL ⟨2⟩　TEACHER D a v i d　W a l k e r

ROOM ⟨2⟩⟨0⟩⟨1⟩

2. Write about Eve.

a.　Her name is Eve Duval. _____

b.　She is from _____

c.　Her first language is _____

d.　_____

e.　_____

f.　_____

g.　Her teacher is _____

h.　_____

Capitalization and Punctuation   **Levels A and B**

**1. Put in capital letters.
Add punctuation.**

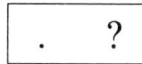

Sara: W̶here are you from, T̶rong?

Trong: i'm from vietnam

Sara: is your first language french

Trong: no, it's not

               my first language is vietnamese

Sara: are you married

Trong: no, i'm not

Sara: how old are you

Trong: i'm 21

2. Copy the interview in 1.

Sara: Where are you from, Trong? _____

Trong: _____

Sara: _____

Trong: _____

Sara: _____

Trong: _____

Sara: _____

Trong: _____

Game: Word Search

1. Find these words:

a.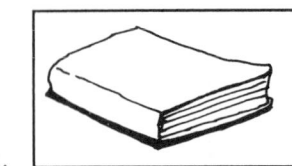

b.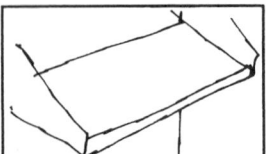

c.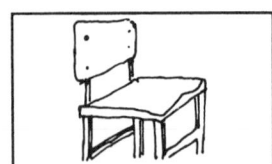

d.

e.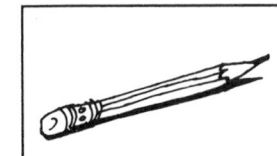

f.

A	D	O	O	R	C	G	T	B	E
C	L	E	P	E	N	C	I	L	Y
V	E	P	C	L	O	C	K	W	I
N	O	T	E	B	O	O	K	E	Y
A	P	B	E	C	H	A	I	R	B
M	A	R	W	I	N	D	O	W	L
C	L	O	D	E	S	K	A	R	D
A	R	T	V	L	O	C	P	E	N
T	H	O	(B	O	O	K)	E	R	M
R	T	C	O	P	S	H	E	L	F

g.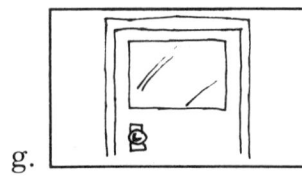

i.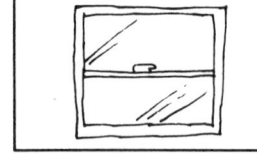

h.

j.

2. Write the words in 1.

a. ___book___

b. _____

c. _____

d. _____

e. _____

f. _____

g. _____

h. _____

i. _____

j. _____

UNIT 4

Grammar

Level A

---

1. Circle.

a. $\boxed{\begin{array}{c} a \\ \textcircled{an} \end{array}}$ accident

b. $\boxed{\begin{array}{c} a \\ an \end{array}}$ fire

c. $\boxed{\begin{array}{c} a \\ an \end{array}}$ apartment

d. $\boxed{\begin{array}{c} a \\ an \end{array}}$ emergency

e. $\boxed{\begin{array}{c} a \\ an \end{array}}$ phone

f. $\boxed{\begin{array}{c} a \\ an \end{array}}$ mailbox

2. Circle.

a. Where is the accident?

   1. Between Second Avenue and State Street.

   2. On the corner of Second Avenue and State Street.

   3. On the corner of First Avenue and State Street.

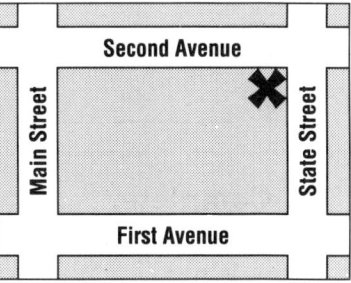

b. Where is the phone?

   1. On the corner of First Avenue and State Street.

   2. On the corner of Main Street and Second Avenue.

   3. Between First Avenue and State Street.

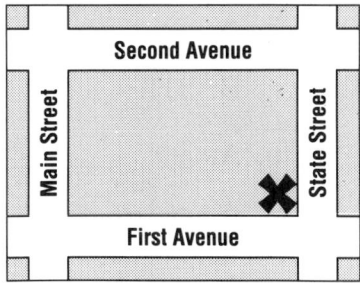

c. Where is the post office?

   1. Between Second Avenue and First Avenue.

   2. On the corner of Second Avenue and Main Street.

   3. On the corner of First Avenue and State Street.

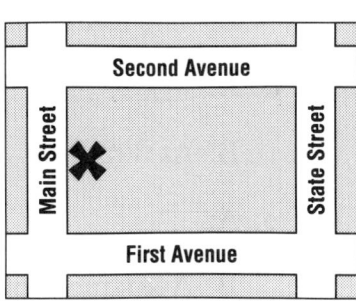

Grammar

1. Complete.

a	an

a. _____an_____ accident

b. _____ fire

c. _____ apartment

d. _____ emergency

e. _____ phone

f. _____ building

g. _____ ambulance

h. _____ mailbox

2. Complete.

What	Where

a. A: _____What_____ is the phone number?

B: 911.

b. A: _____ is a phone?

B: On the corner.

c. A: _____ floor?

B: The fourth floor.

d. A: _____ are you?

B: At 302 First Avenue.

e. A: _____ apartment?

B: Apartment 5G.

(Continued on page 27)

Grammar

3. Answer.

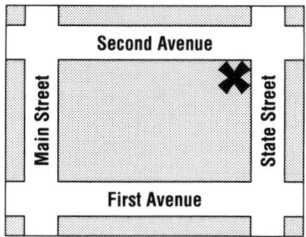

a. Where is the accident?

On the corner of Second Avenue and State Street.

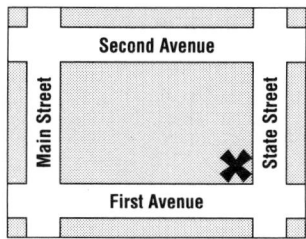

b. Where is the phone?

_____

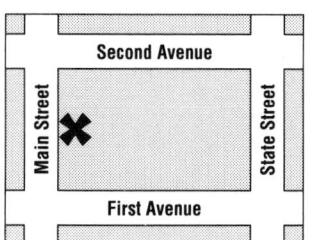

c. Where is the post office?

_____

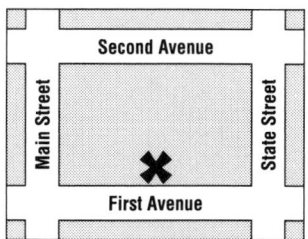

d. Where is the hospital?

_____

Writing   Level A

1. Underline **Address**.

☐ **Please send a one-year gift subscription in my name to:**
☐ I enclose $20 for each subscription.   ☐ Bill me later.
NAME _____ (please print)
ADDRESS _____
CITY _____   STATE _____   ZIP _____
☐ **I'm moving. My new address is:**
NAME _____ (please print)
ADDRESS _____
CITY _____   STATE _____   ZIP _____
Please include label with old address

2. Circle (City).

In case of emergency, notify:

_____

Relation to you: _____

Address:

_____
Street   Apartment

_____
City   State   ZIP Code

Phone: (_____)_____

(Continued on page 29)

Writing

Level A (continued)

3. Circle (City).

   Underline State.

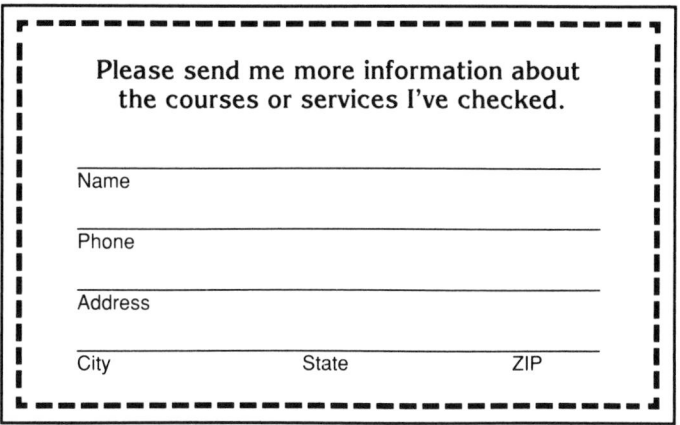

4. Circle (ZIP Code).

UNITED STATES POSTAL SERVICE

OFFICIAL BUSINESS

SENDER INSTRUCTIONS
Print your name, address and ZIP code in the space below.
• Complete items 1, 2, 3, and 4 on the reverse.
• Attach to front of article if space permits, otherwise affix to back of article
• Endorse article "Return Receipt Requested" adjacent to number.

PENALTY FOR PRIVATE USE, $300

U.S.MAIL ®

RETURN TO →

Print Sender's name, address, and ZIP Code in the space below.

5. Complete 3.

Writing   **Level B**

1. Match.

a. name   93205

b. relation   60

c. country   mother

d. age   389 West Street

e. address   975-8134

f. ZIP code   (209)

g. phone number   Kristina Kubiak

h. area code   Poland

2. Write about Kristina Kubiak.
Use the information in 1.

a. Her name is   Kristina Kubiak _____.

b. She is Anna's _____.

c. Kristina is from _____.

d. She _____.

e. Her _____.

f. Her _____.

g. _____.

h. _____.

3. Write about someone in your family.
Use 2 as an example.

a. _____ name is _____.

b. _____ is my _____.

(Continued on page 31)

Writing

Level B (continued)

c. _____

d. _____

e. _____

f. _____

g. _____

h. _____

Capitalization and Punctuation

Levels A and B

1. **a. Circle the apostrophes (').**
   b. Put in capital letters.

   Sara: A̸nna, who can we call in an emergency?

   Anna: oh! call my mother.

   Sara: what's your mother's name?

   Anna: kristina kubiak.

   Sara: how do you spell her last name?

   Anna: it's kubiak. k-u-b-i-a-k.

   Sara: and what's her phone number?

   Anna: it's (209) 975-8134.

2. **Copy the conversation in 1.**

   Sara: <u>Anna, who can we call in an emergency?</u>

   Anna: _____

   Sara: _____

   Anna: _____

   Sara: _____

   Anna: _____

   Sara: _____

   Anna: _____

Game: Where's the fire?

Levels A and B

1. **Look at the picture. Circle all the fires.**

2. **Write the locations of the fires in 1.**

the library
_____   _____

_____   _____

_____   _____

_____

Name _____

School _____

1. Complete.

a. (__I'm__ looking for tissues.)

b. __She's__ looking for toothpaste.

c. _____ looking for shampoo.

d. (_____ looking for aspirin.)

e. ____ _____ ____ Band-Aids.

f. (____ _____ ____ soap.)

(Continued on page 35)

Grammar

2. Complete.

is   are

a. How much _____*are*_____ the tissues?

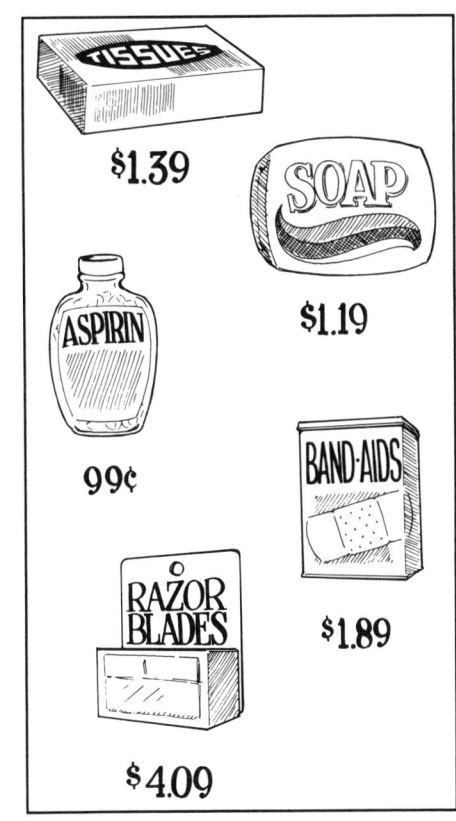

b. How much _____ the soap?

c. How much _____ the aspirin?

d. How much _____ the Band-Aids?

e. How much _____ the razor blades?

3. Answer the questions in 2.

It's   They're

a. _____They're $1.39_____ .

b. _____ .

c. _____ .

d. _____ .

e. _____ .

Grammar
Level B

1. Complete.

a. (I'm looking for tissues.)

b. She's looking for shampoo.

c. _____

d. (_____)

e. _____

f. (_____)

(Continued on page 37)

Grammar

Level B (continued)

2. Complete.

a. A: How much ___is the aspirin___?

B: ___It's 99¢___.

b. A: How much _____?

B: _____.

c. A: How much _____?

B: _____.

d. A: How much _____?

B: _____.

e. A: How much _____?

B: _____.

f. A: How much _____?

B: _____.

Writing

1. Circle (Price). Underline Total.

BOOK CENTER

TO ORDER NOW CALL
1-800-555-0316
or mail this coupon to:

BOOK CENTER
245 Avenue D
New Haven, Connecticut 06516

Qty.	Order No.	Title	Price

Subtotal ____

Add 8% Sales Tax ____

Shipping & Handling ____

$3.50 first item, 75¢ each additional item ____

Total ____

Acct. No. _____

Expiration _____

Name _____

Phone _____

Address (Apt.) _____

City	State	Zip

Signature _____

**Check, Money Order or Charge Card No.
Must Accompany All Orders**

a.

FASTER WINE & SPIRITS

COTE DE BEAUNE 87	1 @ 17.99	17.99
SUB-TOT		17.99
TAX		1.48
TOTAL		19.47
AMT TEND		20.47
CHANGE		1.00

THANK YOU

b.

ISBN	TITLE	QUAN.	PRICE	TOTAL

c.

(Continued on page 39)

Writing
Level A (continued)

2. Check (✓) Money Order.

┌ ─ ─ ─ **Please check one** ─ ─ ─ ─ ─ ─ ─ ─ ─ ─ ─ ─ ─ ┐

☐ FIRM ORDER – Please indicate method of payment

    ☐ Check ☐ Money Order ☐ MasterCard* ☐ VISA*

☐ C.O.D.

*Account Number _____

*Expiration Date _____ *Signature _____

☐ 30-DAY EXAMINATION ORDER – **SIGNATURE REQUIRED**
I understand that the materials I have requested will be
forwarded with an invoice. I agree to pay the invoice or return
the materials within 30 days of the invoice date.

Signature _____

Minimum Order: Orders totaling less than $20 will be charged an
additional handling fee of $1.50.

3. Check (✓) Check.

┌ ─ ─ ─ **Please check one** ─ ─ ─ ─ ─ ─ ─ ─ ─ ─ ─ ─ ─ ┐

☐ FIRM ORDER – Please indicate method of payment

    ☐ Check ☐ Money Order ☐ MasterCard* ☐ VISA*

☐ C.O.D.

*Account Number _____

*Expiration Date _____ *Signature _____

☐ 30-DAY EXAMINATION ORDER – **SIGNATURE REQUIRED**
I understand that the materials I have requested will be
forwarded with an invoice. I agree to pay the invoice or return
the materials within 30 days of the invoice date.

Signature _____

Minimum Order: Orders totaling less than $20 will be charged an
additional handling fee of $1.50.

4. Look at 1a.
Write your name, phone number, address, city, state, and ZIP Code in 1a.
Sign your name.

Writing

Level B

1. **Read the form.**
   Write the Total.

ORDER FORM

Bob's Book Barn
65 Beacon Street
Boston, Massachusetts 02115

ITEM: PRICE:

  Book #4293 $24.86

  Book #6839   15.64

TOTAL:

Method of payment: ☑ Check ☐ Money Order

Name: Anna Johnson

Address: 4210 Chester Street

         Houston, Texas 77007

---

2. **Write about Anna.**
   Answer these questions.

   a. Where does Anna live?

   b. What is she doing?

   c. Where is Bob's Book Barn?

   d. How is she paying?

   e. What is the total?

   Anna lives _____

   _____

   _____

   _____

   _____

Punctuation

1. Add punctuation. ┌───────┐
│ .   ? │
└───────┘

Add apostrophes. ┌─────┐
│   , │
└─────┘

Pablo: Hi, Carl. Are you busy?

Carl: No What's up

Pablo: Im buying a picture dictionary

Is this order form OK

Carl: Are you paying with a check or a money order

Pablo: With a money order

Carl: Im putting an X in this box

And the total is $6.50

Now its fine

Pablo: Thanks, Carl

Carl: Youre welcome

2. Copy the conversation in 1.

Pablo: ___Hi, Carl. Are you busy?_____

Carl: _____

Pablo: _____

_____

Carl: _____

Pablo: _____

Carl: _____

_____

_____

Pablo: _____

Carl: _____

Game: Word Search

1. Find these words.

 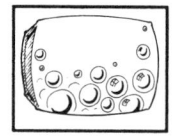 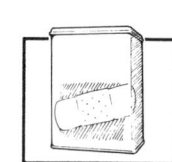 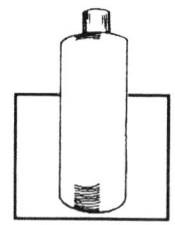  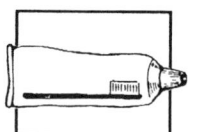

AISLE 1

```
A  M  T  R  O  S  B  I  C  H
F  C  Y  Y  B  W  I  C  W  M
T  R  E  S  O  A  P  B  H  E
D  R  U  G  S  T  O  R  E  S
S  I  C  K  N  O  S  E  M  E
I  T  S  H  A  M  P  O  O  L
R  O  S  E  F  L  O  W  E  R
S  E  E  V  E  R  Y  S  H  E
D  C  B  O  M  W  D  V  R  S
C  H  E  S  T  R  E  A  D  S
```

AISLE 2

```
S  T  R  E  E  T  C  Y  C  W
A  W  V  E  A  T  C  V  M  E
H  A  N  D  J  O  E  H  I  S
A  T  I  S  S  U  E  S  O  N
S  C  H  O  O  L  R  O  O  M
T  H  I  S  R  X  Y  O  U  R
B  A  N  D  A  I  D  S  I  T
R  I  C  H  A  R  D  O  O  R
C  H  I  N  S  O  W  E  A  R
B  R  E  A  D  C  E  N  T  R
```

AISLE 3

```
J  O  C  S  G  T  H  B  O  U
C  A  T  M  A  R  M  E  D  I
S  H  E  G  O  E  S  T  O  T
B  U  Y  W  A  K  E  U  P  I
H  O  W  A  R  E  Y  O  U  R
T  O  O  T  H  P  A  S  T  E
C  O  A  T  S  T  R  E  E  T
T  I  M  E  B  R  X  W  M  O
B  A  S  P  I  R  I  N  O  E
P  M  A  M  C  H  A  I  R  S
```

UNIT 6

Grammar

Level A

1. Match.

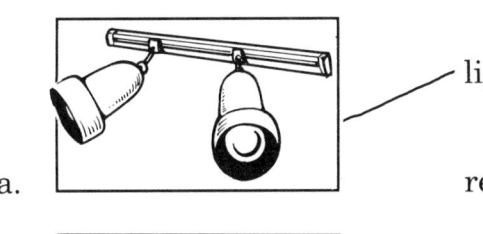

a.

lights

refrigerator

b.

stove

doorbell

d.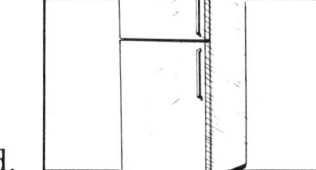

c.

e.

heat

shower

f.

2. Complete.

| isn't working   aren't working |

a.   The ___stove___ ___isn't___ ___working___ .

b.   The _____ _____ _____ .

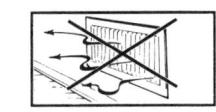

c.   The _____ _____ _____ .

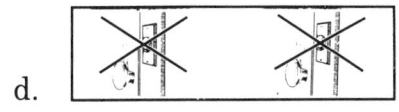

d.   The _____ _____ _____ .

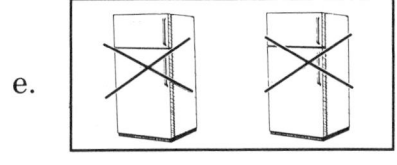

e.   The _____ _____ _____ .

(Continued on page 44)

Grammar

3. **Complete the questions.**
   Circle the correct answer.

a. 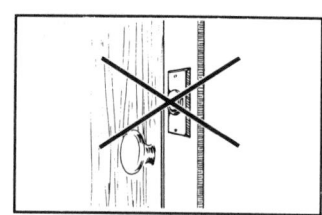 Is the ____doorbell____ working?   Yes, it is.

   No, it isn't.

b.  Are the _____ working?   Yes, they are.

   No, they aren't.

c.  Is the _____ working?   Yes, it is.

   No, it isn't.

d.  _____Is_____ she cooking?   Yes, she is.

   No, she isn't.

e.  _____ they eating dinner?   Yes, they are.

   No, they aren't.

f.  _____ he taking a message?   Yes, he is.

   No, he isn't.

Grammar

Level B

1. Complete.

a.

A: __Are__ __they__ eating dinner?

B: __No__, __they__ __aren't__.

b.

A: _____ _____ cooking dinner?

B: _____, _____ _____.

c.

A: _____ _____ _____ to the drugstore?

B: _____, _____ _____.

d.

A: _____ _____ fixing the stove?

B: _____, _____ _____.

e.

A: _____ YOU waiting for dinner?

B: _____, _____ _____.

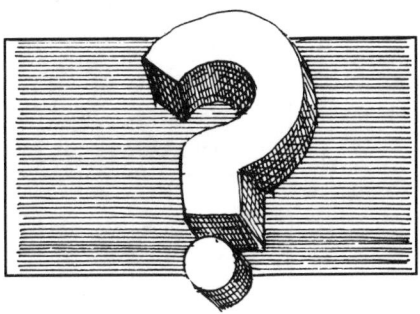

(Continued on page 46)

Grammar

2. **Write a sentence under each picture.**

a.

The lights aren't working.

b.

_____

c.

_____

d.

_____

3. **Complete.**

What is he/she doing?

What are they doing?

a.    They are going to the bank.

b.    _____

c.    _____

d.    _____

e.   _____

Name _____

Address _____

Apartment _____

Writing

Level A

1. Circle (City).
   Underline State.

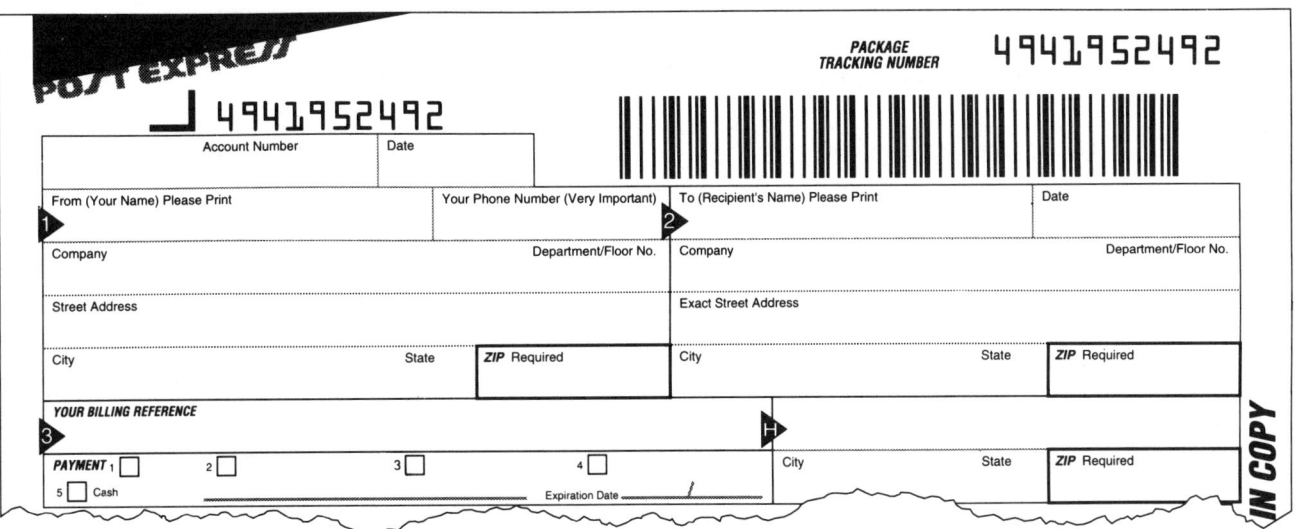

2. Circle (ZIP Code).
   Underline Social Security number.

1. Tell us about yourself

| ☐ Mr. ☐ Miss | First Name | Initial | Last Name | | |
| ☐ Mrs. ☐ Ms. | | | | | |

| Address (to which you want your billing mailed) | Apt. # | City | State | Zip Code |
| Residence Address | Apt. # | City | State | Zip Code |

| Home Phone | Business Phone | Social Security Number | Age | Number of Dependents (excluding Applicant) |

| Are you a United States citizen? ☐ Yes ☐ No | If no, state immigration status | Are you a permanent resident? ☐ Yes ☐ No |

| How long at present address? Yrs. Mos. | ☐ Own ☐ Rent ☐ Board ☐ Live with parents | Monthly Rent or Mortgage Payments $ |

| Former Address (if less than 2 years at present address) | How long? Yrs. Mos. |

Spouse Information

THE INFORMATION BELOW IS REQUIRED IF (1) YOUR SPOUSE IS AN AUTHORIZED BUYER, (2) YOU RESIDE IN A COMMUNITY PROPERTY STATE (AZ, CA, ID, LA, NV, NM, TX, WA, WI), OR (3) YOU ARE RELYING ON THE INCOME OF ANOTHER PERSON AS A SOURCE FOR PAYMENT.

| Name of Spouse | Address | Age |
| Employer | Address | |

| How long? Yrs. Mos. | Occupation | Social Security Number | Net Income (Take Home Pay)$ | ☐ Monthly ☐ Weekly |

3. Look at 1. Write your name, address, city, state, and ZIP Code.
   Look at 2. Write your name and Social Security number.

Writing   Level B

---

1. Read the questions. Circle the letter of the correct answer.

1. Who is Pablo Garcia?

   (a.) A building manager.

   b. In Apartment 1H.

2. Where is he?

   a. Fine, thanks.

   b. In Mrs. Brown's apartment.

3. What is he doing?

   a. He is fixing the refrigerator.

   b. Yes, he is.

4. What's the problem?

   a. It's in the kitchen.

   b. The refrigerator isn't working.

5. Where is Mrs. Brown?

   a. She's in the kitchen.

   b. She's a student.

6. Is she cooking dinner?

   a. No, she isn't.

   b. Mrs. Brown.

7. Is she talking to Pablo?

   a. Yes, she is.

   b. Yes, he is.

2. Write about Pablo and Mrs. Brown. Use the information in 1.

1. Pablo Garcia   is a building manager. _____

2. He's   _____

3. Pablo   _____

4. The refrigerator   _____

5. Mrs. Brown   _____

6. She's   _____

7. _____ to Pablo.

Name ______________________

Date ______________________

Punctuation

Levels A and B

1. Put in capital letters. Add punctuation.

. ?

T
~~t~~uesday, january 15

mr. edwards,

my stove isn't working

are the lights working

please come to apartment 5j

thanks

carmen soto

2. Copy the message in 1.

Tuesday, January 15

Game: "B" Search

Levels A and B

1. Look at the picture. Write all the words that begin with _b_.

bedroom	_____	_____
_____	_____	_____
_____	_____	_____
_____	_____	_____
_____	_____	_____

UNIT 7

Grammar

Level A

1. Complete.

| do the laundry | watch TV | go to the park | play ~~cards~~ |

| do | don't |

a. Do you __play cards__? — No, I __don't__.

b. Do you _____? — Yes, I _____.

c. Do you _____? — Yes, I _____.

d. Do you _____? — No, I _____.

(Continued on page 52)

Grammar

Level A (continued)

2. **Write about yourself.**
   Look at the pictures. Circle Yes or No.
   Complete the sentences.

a. Yes (No) I _don't go to school_ on Sunday.

b. Yes No I _____ on Sunday.

c. Yes No I _____ on Saturday.

d. Yes No I _____ on Monday evening.

e. Yes No I _____ on Saturday.

Grammar

Level B

1. Complete.

a. Do you play cards on Sunday?   Yes, I do.

b. _____ on Friday morning?   _____

c. _____ on Friday or Saturday night?   _____

d. _____ on Tuesday?   _____

Writing

1. Circle (Monday).

   Underline Thursday.

Channel 8 Daytime Schedule

WEEKDAYS

7:00	**NEWS** (Monday–Thursday) **The Seventh Hour** (Friday)
8:00	**Crossroads** (Monday, Wednesday, Friday)
	Jobs Today (Thursday, Friday)
8:30	**Inside Africa**
9:30	**Learn to Read**
10:00	**All About Movies**
11:00	Monday **Beginning French**
	Tuesday **Beginning Spanish**
	Wednesday **Beginning Korean**
	Thursday **Beginning Chinese**
	Friday **Beginning Vietnamese**
12:00	**The Twelfth Hour** (except Monday)
	Weekend Review (Monday)

2. Circle (Social Security number).

Form **1040A**	Department of the Treasury—Internal Revenue Service **U.S. Individual Income Tax Return** (O) **1992**	
Step 1 **Label** Use IRS label. Otherwise, please print or type.	L A B E L H E R E Your first name and initial Last name If a joint return, spouse's first name and initial Last name Home address (number and street). (If you have a P.O. box, see page 15 of instructions.) Apt. no. City, town or post office, state and ZIP code. (If you have a foreign address, see page 7.)	OMB No. 1545-0085 Your social security number Spouse's social security number **For Privacy Act and Paperwork Reduction Act Notice, see page 3.**

3. Look at 2. Write your Social Security number.

Writing

1. **Complete your schedule for Monday. Write the time.**

☐		**March 11**
☐	8 : 00	MONDAY
☐	:	
☐	:	
☐	:	
☐	:	
☐	:	
☐	:	
☐	8 : 00	

2. **Write about your Monday schedule.**

This is my Monday schedule.

At _____ , I _____
(time)

_____

_____

_____

_____

_____

_____

_____

Capitalization and Punctuation

Levels A and B

1. **Put in capital letters.**
   Add punctuation.

.	?

   A: ~~d~~Do you want to play cards on ~~w~~Wednesday evening ?

   B: oh, i'm sorry

       i'm not free on wednesday

       how about thursday evening

   A: i'm sorry

       i work on thursday

       are you free friday evening

   B: what time

   A: how about 7:30

   B: that's fine

2. **Copy the conversation in 1.**

   A: _Do you want to play cards on Wednesday evening?_

   B: _____

   _____

   _____

   A: _____

   _____

   _____

   B: _____

   A: _____

   B: _____

Crossword Puzzle   **Levels A and B**

1. **Write the seven days of the week.**

   a. <u>Monday</u>   e. _____

   b. _____   f. _____

   c. _____   g. _____

   d. _____

2. **Complete with the seven days.**

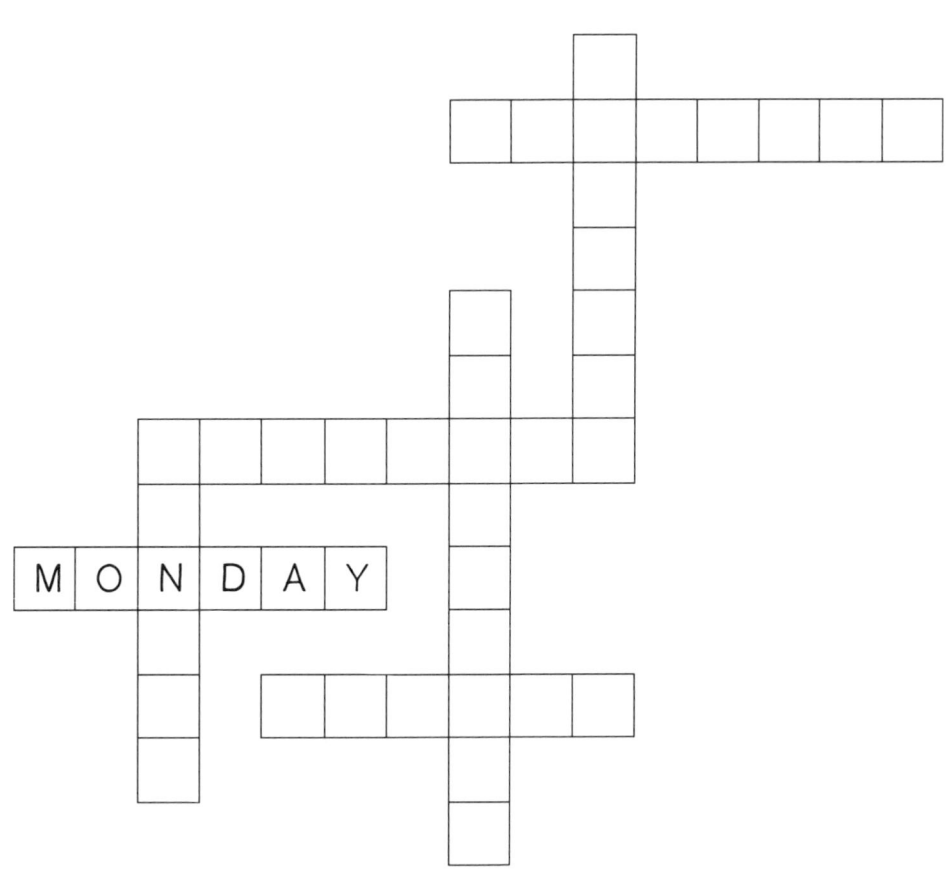

Name _____
First   Middle Initial   Last

Grammar   Level A

1. Circle.

a.   Does he feel sick?   Yes, he does.
                                           No, he doesn't.

b.   Does she have a toothache?   Yes, she does.
                                           No, she doesn't.

c.   Does she feel dizzy?   Yes, she does.
                                           No, she doesn't.

d.   Does he have an earache?   Yes, he does.
                                           No, he doesn't.

2. Complete.

a.   Does _____ he _____ have a headache?

b.   _____ she feel tired?

c.   Does she _____ a stomachache?

d.   _____ he have a sore throat?

(Continued on page 59)

Grammar

Level A (continued)

3. Answer the questions in 2.

a. ___Yes, he does._____

b. _____

c. _____

d. _____

4. Complete.

| has   doesn't have |

a. He _____has_____ a fever.

b. She _____ a toothache.

c. She _____ a headache.

d. He _____ an earache.

e. She _____ a cold.

Grammar   Level B

1. Write questions.

| have   feel |

a. nauseous?

Does he feel nauseous?

b. a fever?

c. a backache?

d. tired?

e. a headache?

(Continued on page 61)

Grammar   Level B (continued)

2. Answer the questions in 1.

a. _Yes, he does._ _____

b. _____

c. _____

d. _____

e. _____

3. Look at the doctor's notes. Write sentences about Laura. Use the words in parentheses ( ).

> **Dr. Tahira Homayun**
> 2001 University Avenue
> Madison, Wisconsin 53705
>
> Laura Banks
>
> -flu
> -headache
> -no stomachache
> -sore throat
> -no fever

a. (well) _She doesn't feel well._ _____

b. (flu) _____

c. (headache) _____

d. (stomachache) _____

e. (sore throat)_____

f. (fever) _____

Crossword Puzzle

Down ↓

1.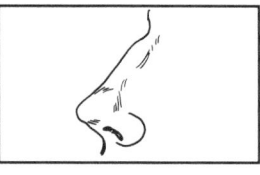

2.

3.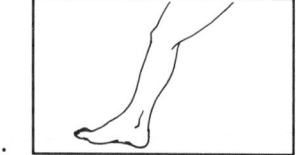

4.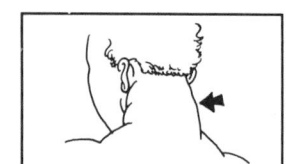

7.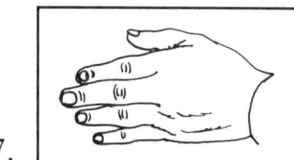

10.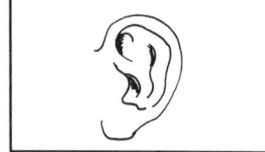

11.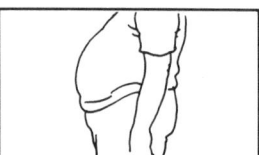

13.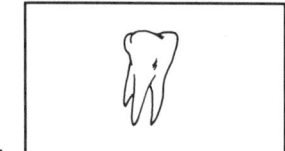

Across →

5.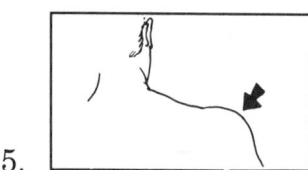

6.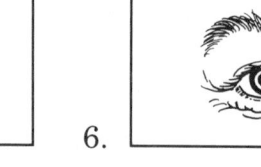

8.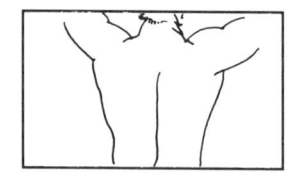

9.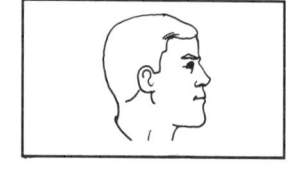

12.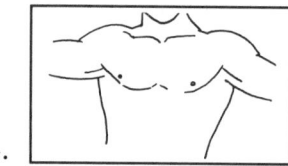

14.

Writing

Level A

1. Circle (initial).

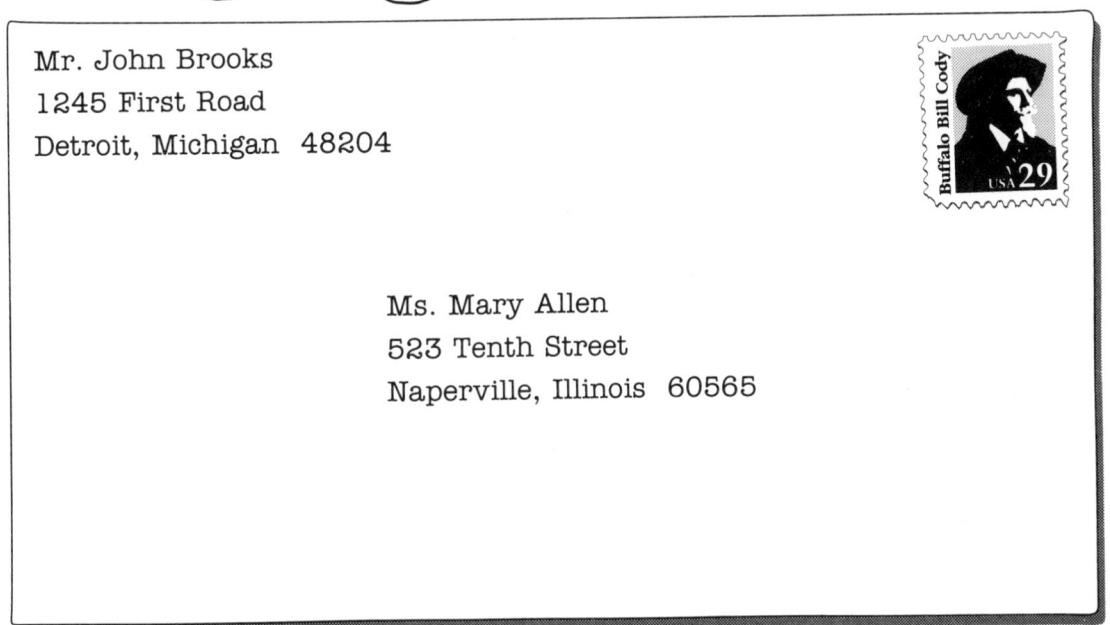

2. Underline <u>Ms.</u> Circle (Mr.)

Mr. John Brooks
1245 First Road
Detroit, Michigan 48204

Ms. Mary Allen
523 Tenth Street
Naperville, Illinois 60565

3. Look at 1.
Write your name, your address, and your Social Security number.

Writing   Level B

1. Read about Alba Burgos.

Name __Alba Burgos_____

Age __45_____

Marital Status __Married_____

Children? __1 daughter_____

cold	(yes)	no
headache	(yes)	no
sore throat	(yes)	no
fever	yes	(no)
need prescription?	yes	(no)

2. Write about Alba.

__Alba Burgos is_____ 45 years old.

She _____ married.

She _____ one daughter.

_____ well.

_____ a cold.

Her head _____.

She _____ a sore throat.

She _____ a fever.

Alba _____ a prescription.

Capitalization

Levels A and B

1. Put in capital letters.

M L   F C
ms. lucia f. chen

107 first street

new york, new york 10009

         mr. roberto m. rodriguez

         421 western avenue

         los angeles, california 90004

2. Copy 1.

Ms. Lucia F. Chen

UNIT 9

Last Name _____

[ ] Male   [ ] Female   (check one)

Grammar

Level A

1. Complete.

do	does

a. Where __do__ I get off?   Fourth Avenue.

b. Where _____ she get off?   3rd Street.

c. Where _____ we get off?   Union Park.

d. Where _____ they get off?   First Avenue.

e. Where _____ he get off?   2nd Street.

f. Where _____ you get off?   City Hall.

2. Answer the questions in 1.

get off	gets off

a. You _____ get off _____ at _____ Fourth Avenue _____.

b. She _____ at _____.

c. We _____ at _____.

d. They _____ at _____.

e. He _____ at _____.

f. I _____ at _____.

(Continued on page 67)

Grammar

Level A (continued)

3. **Where does this bus go? Answer the question.**

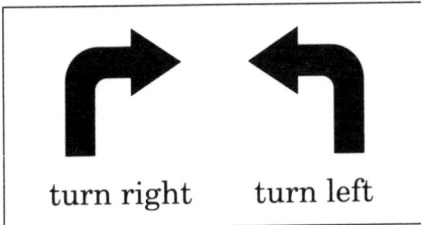

turn right   turn left

First Street

It turns right on First Street.

a.

Second Avenue

_____

b.

Union Street

_____

c.

Vermont Street

_____

d.

Fifth Avenue

_____

e.

Grammar

**1. Complete the conversations.
Use the words in parentheses ( ).**

Marie: Excuse me. Does this bus _____go_____ to the train station?
                                                             a. (go)

Bus driver: Yes, it _____.
                                    b. (do)

Marie: Where do I _____?
                                          c. (get off)

Bus driver: Get off at Fifth Street.

Carmen: _____ the Number 5 bus _____ here?
                         d. (do)   e. (stop)

Bus driver: No, it _____.
                                 f. (do)

                It _____ on Fourth Street.
                      g. (stop)

Han Fu: How _____ I _____ to Union Park?
                         h. (do)   i. (get)

Bus driver: _____ one block and _____ left.
                      j. (go)   k. (turn)

Han Fu: Thanks.

(Continued on page 69)

Grammar

2. **Complete the questions about the people in 1.**

Where	How	What

a. _____Where_____ does Marie want to go?

b. _____ number bus does Carmen take?

c. _____ does Carmen's bus stop ?

d. _____ does Han Fu get to Union Park?

3. **Answer the questions in 2.**

a. _She wants to go to the train station._____

b. _____

c. _____

d. _____

Writing

Level A

1. Circle (bus).

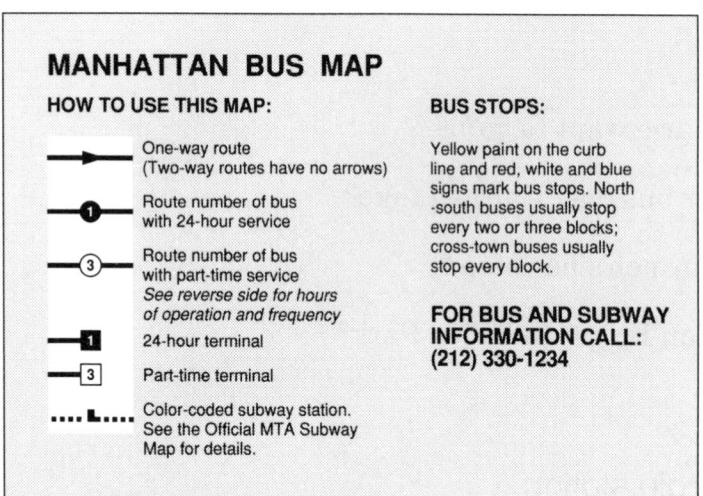

MANHATTAN BUS MAP

HOW TO USE THIS MAP:

➡️ One-way route
(Two-way routes have no arrows)

1 Route number of bus
with 24-hour service

3 Route number of bus
with part-time service
*See reverse side for hours
of operation and frequency*

1 24-hour terminal

3 Part-time terminal

⋯⋯L⋯ Color-coded subway station.
See the Official MTA Subway
Map for details.

BUS STOPS:

Yellow paint on the curb
line and red, white and blue
signs mark bus stops. North
-south buses usually stop
every two or three blocks;
cross-town buses usually
stop every block.

**FOR BUS AND SUBWAY
INFORMATION CALL:**
(212) 330-1234

a.

Places to Visit

American Academy of Arts and Letters, M-2
Audubon Terrace, Broadway at 155th Street
Bus:　　M2, M3, M4, M5, M100, M101; M41, Stop 10
Subway:　1 to 157th Street; AA, B to 155 Street

American Craft Museum, G-4
44 West 53rd Street
See Museum of Modern Art

American Museum of Natural History, H-3
Central Park West at 79th Street
Bus:　　M7, M10, M11, M17, M104; M41, Stop 8
Subway:　1 to 79th Street, AA, B, CC to 81st Street

American Stock Exchange, A-5
86 Trinity Place
Bus:　　M1, M6, M15; B88, Stop 27
Subway:　2, 3 to Wall Street; 4, 5 to Wall St; RR, N to
　　　　Rector Street; J, M to Broad Street

Carnegie Hall, G-4
Seventh Avenue at 57th Street
Bus:　　M5, M6, M7; M10, M28, M30, M32, M103,
　　　　M104; M41, Stop 5
Subway:　Subway 1; A, D, AA, B, CC to 59 Street-
　　　　Columbus Circle; B to 57 Street; D, E,
　　　　to 7 Avenue; RR, N, QB to 57 Street

b.

2. Circle (train).

B	C	R	RIDERS RES. NO.

EXCURSION
ENDORSEMENTS

RIDERS RES. NO.
1　/TD
ACCOM. CHARGE
$.00
ACCOM. CHARGE
$ 87.00
ACCOM. CHARGE
$ 87.00

NOT FOR CARRIAGE

FROM-TO　　DEPARTURE TIME　　TIME
MTR - NYG　　UNRESERVED
FROM-TO
WELCOME ABOARD　　　TRAIN NO.
SPACE/CAR　　　ACCT NUMBER
UNRES COACH　　　CASH

FARE PLAN
BR07
PAY CODE
CA

DATE OF SALE　　TICKET NO.　　NO. OF　　PRICE POINTS
12MAY91　　3325074750　　01 / 01　　NYG-MTR
SUBJECT TO CONDITIONS ON REVERSE

PASSENGER RECEIPT

a.

GOING	RETURNING
Train No. _____	Train No. _____
Date _____	Date _____
Departure Time _____	Departure Time _____
Car/Space _____	Car/Space _____
Arrival Time _____	Arrival Time _____

b.

3. Circle (City).
Underline State.

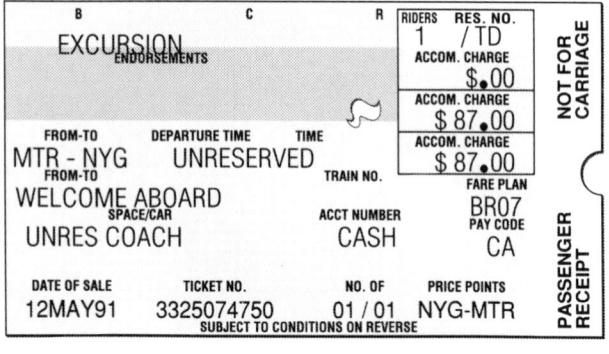

Big trial subscription savings—up to 64% off the single-copy price

Pick your own term (check one box please):

❑ 2 years (48 issues) $69　　　　❑ 1 year (24 issues) $39

Name_____

Address_____

City_____ State_____ Zip_____

4. Complete 3.

Writing   **Level B**

1. Look at the map.

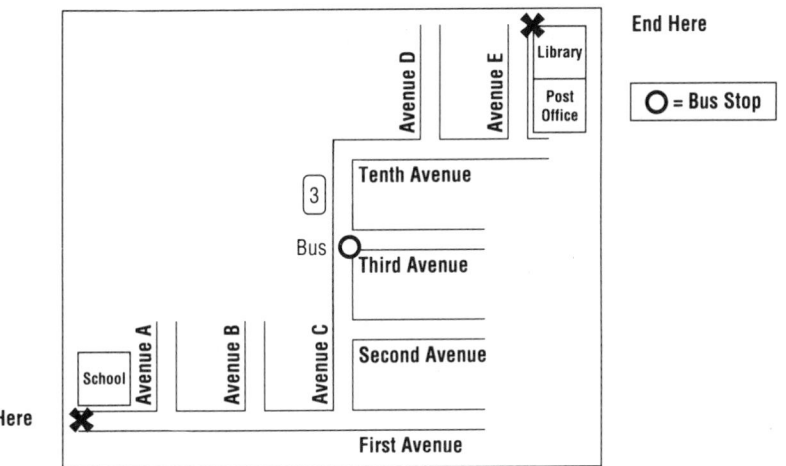

2. Your friend is at school.
He/She asks "How do I get to the library?"
Write directions.

Go straight on First Avenue to ____Avenue____ ____C____ .
                                    a.   b.

_____ _____ on Avenue C.
  c.   d.

Go _____ blocks to _____ Avenue.
    e.   f.

There is a bus stop on the corner.

_____ the Number 3 bus.
  g.

_____ _____ at Tenth Avenue.
  h.   i.

Go straight on _____ _____ to _____ _____ .
            j.   k.   l.   m.

_____ _____ on Avenue E.
  n.   o.

The library is _____ _____ the post office.
        p.   q.

Capitalization

Levels A and B

1. **Put in capital letters.**

   A: E̸xcuse me. how do i get to the library?

   B: go straight on main street to post road. turn left on post road.

   A: turn right on post road?

   B: no. turn left. walk two blocks.

   the library is on the corner of post road and chambers street.

   A: thank you.

2. **Copy the conversation in 1.**

   A: <u>Excuse me. How do I get to the library?</u> _____

   B: _____

   A: _____

   B: _____

   _____

   A: _____

Game: Word Search

1. **Find these words. The words go** ⟶ .

I take the  to school.

My sister doesn't  to work.

Turn at the corner.

Do you have a  ?

Does Ben  to school?

Turn ◤ at Fifth Street.

Where is the  station?

Go ➡ on Second Avenue.

B	E	O	L	E	F	T	O	E	M	Y
W	A	N	T	B	A	N	B	U	S	E
R	E	N	T	A	P	T	B	P	P	K
S	T	R	A	I	G	H	T	P	E	N
H	O	U	R	O	O	T	R	A	I	N
C	L	W	A	L	K	F	L	O	O	R
G	H	O	S	T	D	R	I	V	E	X
A	P	P	L	E	A	S	E	S	A	Y
C	A	T	B	I	K	E	T	I	M	E
T	H	I	S	I	S	R	I	G	H	T

Name _____

(please print)

Date of Birth _____

Grammar

1. Match.

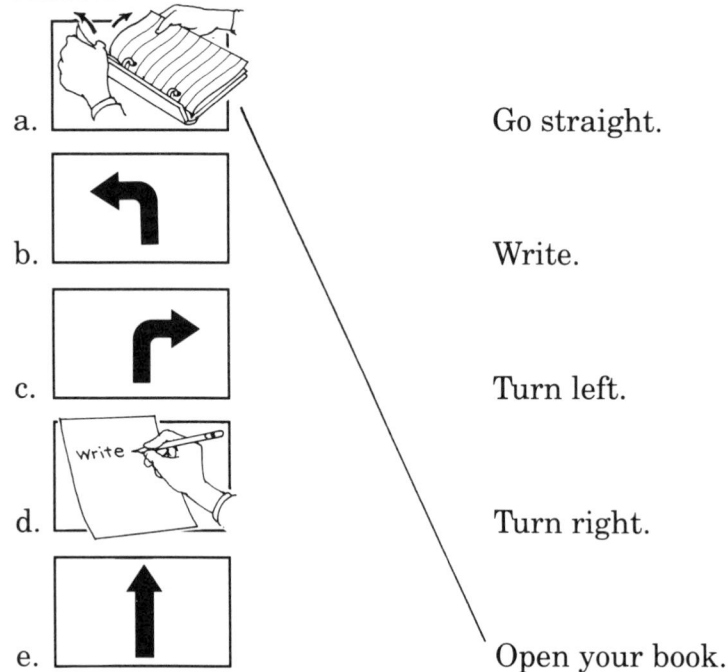

a.

b.

c.

d.

e.

Go straight.

Write.

Turn left.

Turn right.

Open your book.

2. Write a sentence under each picture.

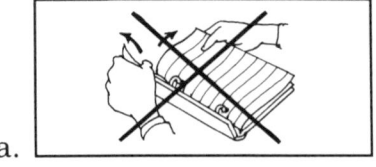

a.

Don't open your book.

b.

c.

d.

e.

(Continued on page 75)

Grammar

Level A (continued)

3. **Write a sentence under each picture.**

a.

Go straight.

b.

Don't turn right.

c.

_____

d.

_____

e.

_____

f.

_____

g.

_____

Grammar

Level B

1. **Complete the sentences.**
   Follow the instructions.

   a. _Don't_ sign your name.

   Print your name.

   _____

   Name (please print)

   b. _____ _____ your name.

   _____ your name.

   _____

   Signature

   c. _____ use a pencil.

   _____ a pen.

   d. _____ write your middle name.

   _____ your middle initial.

   _____

   First   M.I.   Last

   e. _____ put your first name first.

   _____ your last name first.

   _____

   Last   First

   f. _____ put the time in the "In" Box.

   _____ the time in the "Out" Box.

   [   ]   [   ]

   In   Out

   g. _____ underline your marital status.

   _____ your marital status.

   Married   Single

   Divorced   Widowed

   (Circle one.)

Crossword Puzzle

1. Write the twelve months.

a. _____January_____   g. _____

b. _____   h. _____

c. _____   i. _____

d. _____   j. _____

e. _____   k. _____

f. _____   l. _____

2. Complete with the 12 months.

J	A	N	U	A	R	Y									

Writing

1. Circle (Date of Birth).

Underline Signature.

a.

Date of birth: _____/_____/_____

Date of entry to U.S.: _____/_____/_____

_____
Signature

b.

ALL DAY
Deliveries

28 Main Street   312-467-9876

Job Number: _____   Date: _____

BILL TO: _____
PICK-UP: _____
_____

DELIVER: _____

_____

PICK-UP

WAITING TIME: _____   SIGNATURE: _____

WAITING TIME: _____   SIGNATURE: _____

c.

GROUP HEALTH MEDICAL INSURANCE ENROLLMENT FORM

EMPLOYEE

Last Name	First Name	M.I.	Date of Birth

Marital Status: ☐ Single ☐ Married ☐ Separated ☐ Divorced ☐ Widowed

Street Address	Apartment

City	State	ZIP Code

Telephone	Social Security Number	Occupation

d.

Paid Preparer's Use Only	Preparer's signature	Date	Check if self-employed ☐	Sign Here	Your signature	Date
	Firm's name *(or yours if self-employed)*	Preparer's social security number			Spouse's signature *(if joint claim)*	Date
	Firm's address	Employer identification number				

2. Look at 1a. Write your date of birth. Sign your name.
   Look at 1c. Write your name and your date of birth.
   Write your Social Security number.
   Look at 1d. Sign your name.

Signature _____

Date of Birth _____

Writing   Level B

1. Read Alba's health insurance registration form.

EMPLOYEE			
Last Name Sanchez	First Name Alba	M.I. L.	Date of Birth 5/8/61

Marital Status: ☐ Single ☐ Married ☐ Separated ☑ Divorced ☐ Widowed

| Telephone | Social Security Number 938-98-4260 | | Occupation carpenter |

DEPENDENTS					
Last Name	First Name	M.I.	Date of Birth	Social Security Number	Relationship
Sanchez	Ed	R.	2/4/83		
Sanchez	Rosa	M.	8/11/81		

EMPLOYER	
Name The Desk Top	Telephone (213) 556-1313

2. Write about Alba.
Answer these questions.

a. How old is she?

b. What is her marital status?

c. Does she have children?

d. How old are they?

e. What does Alba do?

f. Where does she work?

a. __Alba is_____

b. _____

c. _____

d. _____

e. _____

f. _____

Punctuation

1. Add apostrophes (').

A: What's today's date?

B: Its February 10.

A: February 10? Its Annas birthday!

B: How old is she?

A: I dont know. Twenty-five or twenty-six.

B: Is she in school today?

A: No, she isnt. She doesnt feel well.

B: Whats wrong?

A: She has a headache.

2. Copy the conversation in 1.

What's today's date? _____

_____

_____

_____

_____

_____

_____

_____

Answer Key

UNIT 1

Grammar Level A

Exercise 1
a. She   b. He   c. He   d. She

Exercise 2
a. she's   b. I'm   c. he's   d. you're

Exercise 3
a. His, He's   b. Her, She's   c. His, He's   d. Her, She's

Exercise 4
a. What's   b. What's   c. Where are

Grammar Level B

Exercise 1
a. He's   b. I'm   c. She's   d. You're

Exercise 2
a. I'm   b. I'm   c. He's   d. She's

Exercise 3
a. Her name is Anna.   b. Her name is Neary.
c. His name is Victor.

Exercise 4
a. What's   b. What's   c. Where

Exercise 5
(Answers will vary.)

Writing Level B

Exercise 1
a. name   b. is   c. meet   d. Nice   e. too

Exercise 2
a. Hi.   b. (student's name)   c. your   d. name
e. is   f. meet   g. you   h. Nice   i. to   j. you

Exercise 3
(possible answer)
A: Hi. I'm (student's name). What's your name?
B: My name is Victor.
A: Nice to meet you, Victor.
B: Nice to meet you, too.

Punctuation Levels A and B

Victor: Hi. I'm Victor.
         What's your name?
Anna: My name is Anna.
Victor: I'm from Colombia.
         Where are you from, Anna?
Anna: I'm from Poland.
Victor: Nice to meet you, Anna.
Anna: Nice to meet you, too.

Crossword Puzzle Levels A and B

Exercise 1

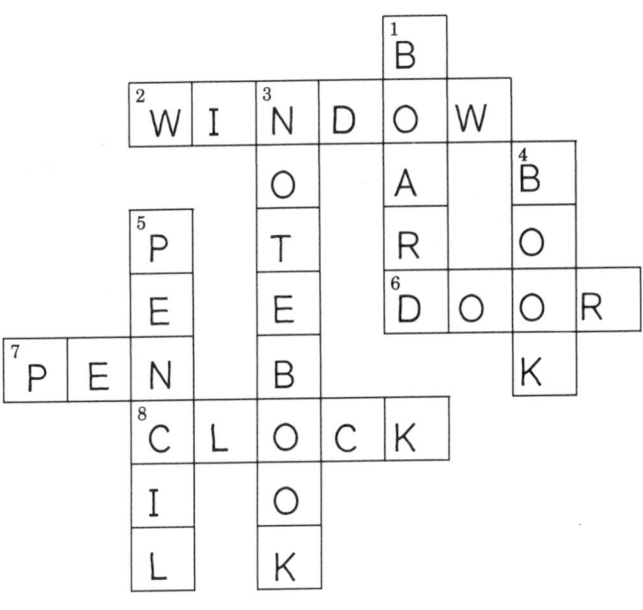

UNIT 2

Grammar Level A

Exercise 1
a. who is   b. that is   c. he is   d. what is
e. they are   f. she is

Exercise 2
a. Who's   b. That's   c. What's   d. she
e. she's   f. Who   g. They're   h. What

Grammar Level B

Exercise 1
a. who's   b. that's   c. what's   d. they're
e. she's   f. he's

Exercise 2
a. Who's   b. that   c. That's   d. What's
e. she's   f. not   g. Yes   h. is

Writing Level B

Exercise 1
a. Who   b. are   c. What   d. are   e. their
f. names   g. Where   h. are   i. they   j. from

Exercise 2
(Answers will vary.)

Exercise 3
(Answers will vary.)

Capitalization Levels A and B

This is my friend.
Her name is Sara Blanca.
She's from Mexico.
This is Ana.
Ana is Sara's daughter.
This is Carlos.
He's Ana's husband.

Crossword Puzzle Levels A and B

UNIT 3

Grammar Level A

Exercise 1
a. It   b. They   c. They   d. It   e. It   f. They
Exercise 2
a. Yes   b. No   c. Yes   d. No
Exercise 3
a. They're   b. It's   c. They're   d. It's

Grammar Level B

Exercise 1
a. No, I'm not.   b. Yes, we are.   c. Yes, I am.
d. No, I'm not.

Exercise 2
(answers will vary)

Exercise 3
a. No   b. I'm   c. not   d. your   e. Are
f. you   g. No   h. I'm   i. not   j. His
k. Where   l. We're   m. it   n. is   o. It's

Writing Level B

(Answers may vary slightly.)
a. Her name is Eve Duval.
b. She is from Haiti.
c. Her first language is Creole.
d. She is single.
e. She is 28 years old.
f. She is in Level 2.
g. Her teacher is David Walker.
h. Her class is in Room 201.

Capitalization and Punctuation Levels A and B

Sara: Where are you from, Trong?
Trong: I'm from Vietnam.
Sara: Is your first language French?
Trong: No, it's not. My first language is Vietnamese.
Sara: Are you married?
Trong: No, I'm not.
Sara: How old are you?
Trong: I'm 21.

Game: Word Search Levels A and B

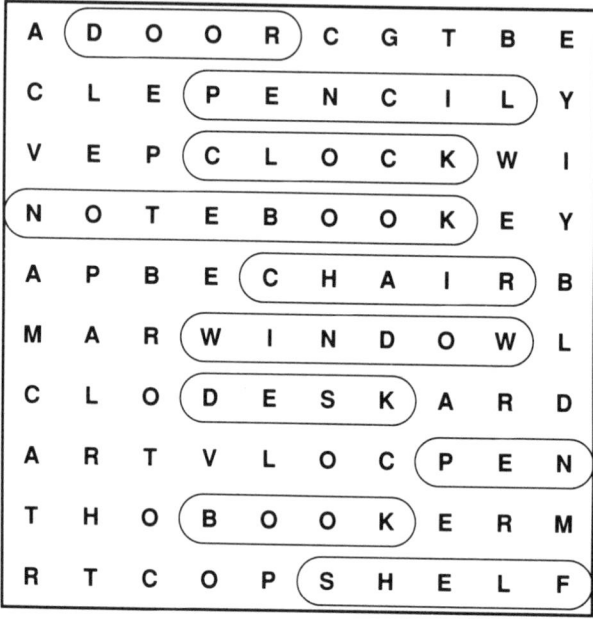

Exercise 2
a. book   b. shelf   c. chair   d. desk   e. pencil
f. pen   g. door   h. clock   i. window
j. notebook

UNIT 4

Grammar Level A

Exercise 1
a. an   b. a   c. an   d. an   e. a   f. a
Exercise 2
a. 2   b. 1   c. 1

Grammar Level B

Exercise 1
a. an   b. a   c. an   d. an   e. a   f. a
g. an   h. a
Exercise 2
a. What   b. Where   c. What   d. Where
e. What
Exercise 3
a. On the corner of Second Avenue and State Street.
b. On the corner of First Avenue and State Street.
c. Between First Avenue and Second Avenue.
d. Between Main Street and State Street.

Writing Level B

Exercise 1
a. Kristina Kubiak   b. mother   c. Poland   d. 60
e. 389 West Street   f. 93205   g. 975-8134
h. (209)

Exercise 2
a. Her name is Kristina Kubiak.
b. She is Anna's mother.
c. Kristina is from Poland.
d. She is 60.
e. Her address is 389 West Street.
f. Her ZIP code is 93205.
g. Her phone number is 975-8134.
h. Her area code is (209).

Exercise 3
(Answers will vary.)

Capitalization and Punctuation Levels A and B

Sara: Anna, who can we call in an emergency?
Anna: Oh! Call my mother.
Sara: What's your mother's name?
Anna: Kristina Kubiak.
Sara: How do you spell her last name?
Anna: It's Kubiak. K-U-B-I-A-K.
Sara: And what's her phone number?
Anna: It's (209) 975-8134.

Game: Where's the fire? Levels A and B

the library, the public phone, the ambulance, the mailbox, 254 Main Street, the police station (statue), on the police station building (poster), the car

UNIT 5

Grammar Level A

Exercise 1
a. I'm   b. She's   c. He's   d. I'm   e. He's
looking for   f. I'm looking for

Exercise 2
a. are   b. is   c. is   d. are   e. are

Exercise 3
a. They're $1.39.   b. It's $1.19.   c. It's 99¢.
d. They're $1.89.   e. They're $4.09.

Grammar Level B

Exercise 1
a. I'm looking for tissues.   b. She's looking for shampoo.   c. He's looking for toothpaste.   d. I'm looking for aspirin.   e. He's looking for Band-Aids.
f. I'm looking for soap.

Exercise 2
a. A: How much is the aspirin?
   B: It's 99¢.
b. A: How much are the tissues?
   B: They're $1.39.
c. A: How much is the toothpaste?
   B: It's $1.79.
d. A: How much are the Band-Aids?
   B: They're $1.89.
e. A: How much is the cold medicine?
   B: It's $3.29.
f. A: How much is the soap?
   B: It's $1.19.

Writing Level B

a. Anna lives in Houston, Texas.
b. She is buying books.
c. Bob's Book Barn is in Boston, Massachusetts.
d. Anna is paying with a check.
e. The total is $40.50.

Punctuation Levels A and B

Pablo: Hi, Carl. Are you busy?
Carl: No. What's up?
Pablo: I'm buying a picture dictionary.
         Is this order form OK?
Carl: Are you paying with a check or a money order?
Pablo: With a money order.
Carl: I'm putting an X in this box.
         And the total is $6.50.
         Now it's fine.
Pablo: Thanks, Carl.
Carl: You're welcome.

Game: Word Search Levels A and B

AISLE 1

A	M	T	R	O	S	B	C	H
F	C	Y	Y	B	W	I	C	W	M
T	R	E	S	O	A	P	B	H	E
D	R	U	G	S	T	O	R	E	S
S	I	C	K	N	O	S	E	M	E
I	T	S	H	A	M	P	O	O	L
R	O	S	E	F	L	O	W	E	R
S	E	E	V	E	R	Y	S	H	E
D	C	B	O	M	W	D	V	R	S
C	H	E	S	T	R	E	A	D	S

AISLE 2

S	T	R	E	E	T	C	Y	C	W
A	W	V	E	A	W	C	V	M	E
H	A	N	D	J	O	E	H	I	S
A	T	I	S	S	U	E	S	O	N
S	C	H	O	O	L	R	O	O	M
T	H	I	S	R	X	Y	O	U	R
B	A	N	D	A	I	D	S	I	T
R	I	C	H	A	R	D	O	O	R
C	H	I	N	S	O	W	E	A	R
B	R	E	A	D	C	E	N	T	R

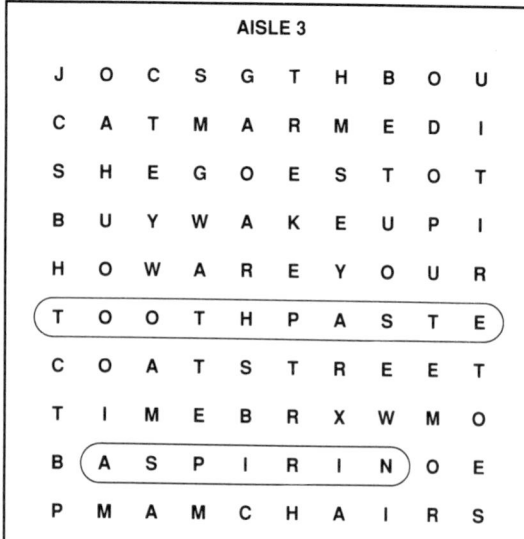

```
                    AISLE 3
J   O   C   S   G   T   H   B   O   U
C   A   T   M   A   R   M   E   D   I
S   H   E   G   O   E   S   T   O   T
B   U   Y   W   A   K   E   U   P   I
H   O   W   A   R   E   Y   O   U   R
(T   O   O   T   H   P   A   S   T   E)
C   O   A   T   S   T   R   E   E   T
T   I   M   E   B   R   X   W   M   O
B  (A   S   P   I   R   I   N)  O   E
P   M   A   M   C   H   A   I   R   S
```

UNIT 6

Grammar Level A

Exercise 1
a. lights   b. stove   c. heat   d. refrigerator
e. doorbell   f. shower

Exercise 2
a. The stove isn't working.
b. The lights aren't working.
c. The heat isn't working.
d. The refrigerators aren't working.
e. The doorbells aren't working.

Exercise 3
a. doorbell   No, it isn't.
b. lights   Yes, they are.
c. stove   Yes, it is.
d. Is   No, she isn't.
e. Are   Yes, they are.
f. Is   Yes, he is.

Grammar Level B

Exercise 1
a. A: Are they eating dinner?
   B: No, they aren't.
b. A: Is he cooking dinner?
   B: No, he isn't.
c. A: Is she going to the drugstore?
   B: Yes, she is.
d. A: Are they fixing the stove?
   B: No, they aren't.
e. A: Are YOU waiting for dinner?
   B: (Answers will vary.)

Exercise 2
a. The lights aren't working.
b. The stove isn't working.
c. The refrigerator isn't working.
d. The doorbell isn't working.

Exercise 3
a. They are going to the bank.
b. He is eating dinner.
c. She is going to the drugstore.
d. They are eating dinner.
e. (Answers will vary.)

Writing Level B

Exercise 1
1. a.   2. b.   3. a.   4. b.   5. a.   6. a.
7. a.

Exercise 2
1. Pablo Garcia is a building manager.
2. He's in Mrs. Brown's apartment.
3. Pablo is fixing the refrigerator.
4. The refrigerator isn't working.
5. Mrs. Brown is in the kitchen.
6. She's not cooking dinner.
7. She's talking to Pablo.

Punctuation Levels A and B

Tuesday, January 15
Mr. Edwards,
My stove isn't working.
Are the lights working?
Please come to Apartment 5J.
Thanks.

Carmen Soto

Game: "B" Search Levels A and B

bedroom, beds, boys, brothers, blackboard, box, bathroom, bathtub, Band-Aids, (razor) blades, book, building, batteries, (dollar) bills

UNIT 7

Grammar Level A

Exercise 1
a. Do you play cards?   No, I don't.
b. Do you do the laundry?   Yes, I do.
c. Do you watch TV?   Yes, I do.
d. Do you go to the park?   No, I don't.

Exercise 2
No   I don't go to school on Sunday. (Other answers will vary.)

Grammar Level B

Exercise 1
a. Do you play cards on Sunday?   Yes, I do.
b. Do you go to school on Friday morning?   No, I don't.
c. Do you watch TV on Friday or
   Saturday night?   Yes, I do.
d. Do you go to the park on Tuesday?   No, I don't.

Exercise 2
(Answers will vary.)

Writing Level B

(Answers will vary.)

Capitalization and Punctuation Levels A and B

A: Do you want to play cards on Wednesday evening?
B: Oh, I'm sorry.
   I'm not free on Wednesday.
   How about Thursday evening?
A: I'm sorry.
   I work on Thursday.
   Are you free Friday evening?
B: What time?
A: How about 7:30?
B: That's fine.

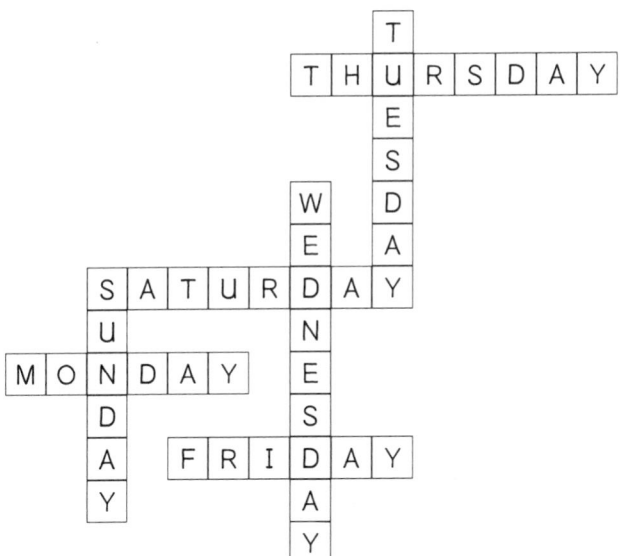

UNIT 8

Grammar Level A

Exercise 1
a. Yes, he does.
b. No, she doesn't.
c. Yes, she does.
d. Yes, he does.

Exercise 2
a. he   b. Does   c. have   d. Does

Exercise 3
a. Yes, he does.
b. Yes, she does.
c. No, she doesn't.
d. No, he doesn't.

Exercise 4
a. has   b. doesn't have   c. doesn't have
d. has   e. has

Grammar Level B

Exercise 1
a. Does he feel nauseous?
b. Does she have a fever?
c. Does he have a backache?
d. Does she feel tired?
e. Does he have a headache?

Exercise 2
a. Yes, he does.
b. Yes, she does.
c. No, he doesn't.
d. Yes, she does.
e. Yes, he does.

Exercise 3
a. She doesn't feel well.
b. She has the flu.
c. She has a headache.

d. She doesn't have a stomachache.
e. She has a sore throat.
f. She doesn't have a fever.

Crossword Puzzle Levels A and B

Writing Level B

Exercise 2
Alba Burgos is 45 years old.
She is married.
She has one daughter.
Alba/She doesn't feel well.
She/Alba has a cold.
Her head hurts.
She has a sore throat.
She doesn't have a fever.
Alba doesn't need a prescription.

Capitalization

Ms. Lucia F. Chen
107 First Street
New York, New York 10009

Mr. Roberto M. Rodriguez
421 Western Avenue
Los Angeles, California 90004

UNIT 9

Grammar Level A

Exercise 1
a. do   b. does   c. do   d. do   e. does
f. do

Exercise 2
a. You get off at Fourth Avenue.
b. She gets off at 3rd Street.
c. We get off at Union Park.
d. They get off at First Avenue.
e. He gets off at 2nd Street.
f. I get off at City Hall.

Exercise 3
a. It turns right on First Street.
b. It turns left on Second Avenue.
c. It turns left on Union Street.
d. It turns right on Vermont Street.
e. It turns right on Fifth Avenue.

Grammar Level B

Exercise 1
a. go   b. does   c. get off   d. Does   e. stop
f. doesn't   g. stops   h. do   i. get   j. Go
k. turn

Exercise 2
a. Where   b. What   c. Where   d. How

Exercise 3
a. She wants to go to the train station.
b. She takes the Number 5 bus.
c. Her bus stops on Fourth Street.
d. He goes one block and turns left.

Writing Level B

Exercise 2
a. Avenue   b. C   c. Turn   d. left   e. two
f. Third   g. Take   h. Get   i. off   j. Tenth
k. Avenue   l. Avenue   m. E   n. Turn   o. left
p. next   q. to

Punctuation Levels A and B

A: Excuse me. How do I get to the library?
B: Go straight on Main Street to Post Road. Turn left on Post Road.
A: Turn right on Post Road?
B: No. Turn left. Walk two blocks.
   The library is on the corner of Post Road and Chambers Street.
A: Thank you.

Game: Word Search Levels A and B

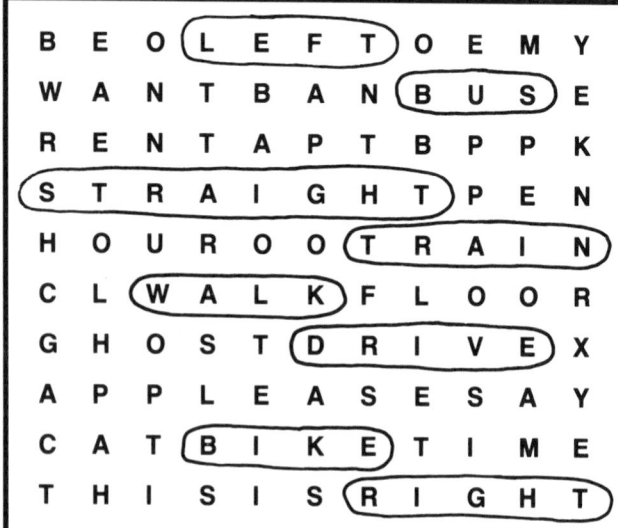

UNIT 10

Grammar Level A

Exercise 1
a. Open your book.   b. Turn left.   c. Turn right.
d. Write.   e. Go straight.

Exercise 2
a. Don't open your book.   b. Don't write.   c. Don't turn right.   d. Don't turn left.   e. Don't go straight.

Exercise 3
a. Go straight.   b. Don't turn right.   c. Don't go straight.   d. Turn left.   e. Don't turn left.   f. Turn right.   g. Don't smoke.

Grammar Level B

Exercise 1
a. Don't, Print   b. Don't print, Sign   c. Don't, Use
d. Don't, Write   e. Don't, Put   f. Don't, Put
g. Don't, Circle

Writing Level B

a. Alba is (age will vary).
b. She is divorced.
c. She has a daughter and a son.
d. Her daughter is (age will vary). Her son is (age will vary).
e. Alba is a carpenter.
f. She works at The Desk Top.

Punctuation Levels A and B

A: What's today's date?
B: It's February 10.
A: February 10? It's Anna's birthday!
B: How old is she?
A: I don't know. Twenty-five or twenty-six.
B: Is she in school today?
A: No, she isn't. She doesn't feel well.
B: What's wrong?
A: She has a headache.

Game: Crossword Puzzle Levels A and B